WITH HONOR AND RESPECT

DAVID SHRECKENGOST

© 2020 David Shreckengost. All rights reserved.

No part of this book may be reproduced, stored in a retrieval system, or transmitted by any means without the written permission of the author.

AuthorHouse™
1663 Liberty Drive
Bloomington, IN 47403
www.authorhouse.com
Phone: 1 (800) 839-8640

Because of the dynamic nature of the Internet, any web addresses or links contained in this book may have changed since publication and may no longer be valid. The views expressed in this work are solely those of the author and do not necessarily reflect the views of the publisher, and the publisher hereby disclaims any responsibility for them.

Any people depicted in stock imagery provided by Getty Images are models, and such images are being used for illustrative purposes only.
Certain stock imagery © Getty Images.

This book is printed on acid-free paper.

ISBN: 978-1-7283-4816-2 (sc)
ISBN: 978-1-7283-4817-9 (hc)
ISBN: 978-1-7283-4818-6 (e)

Library of Congress Control Number: 2020904211

Print information available on the last page.

Published by AuthorHouse 03/12/2020

authorHOUSE

CONTENTS

DEDICATION V
AN INTRODUCTION TO THIS BOOK VI
CHAPTER 1   1
CHAPTER 2   THE 'TEMPORARY' RIDE CAPTAIN 21
CHAPTER 3   RIDE CAPTAIN 33
CHAPTER 4   HERE, THERE, AND EVERYWHERE 41
CHAPTER 5   ANOTHER YEAR 53
CHAPTER 6   IT WAS A BAD YEAR 73
CHAPTER 7   IT WAS A DIFFERENT KIND OF YEAR 85
CHAPTER 8   CLOSER TO HOME 107
CHAPTER 9   ANOTHER YEAR OF HONORING HEROES 119
CHAPTER 10   THE BUSIEST YEAR YET 133
CHAPTER 11   THIS ONE HIT REALLY CLOSE TO HOME 165
CHAPTER 12   THE MISSION CONTINUES – 189

DEDICATION

This book is dedicated to my friend and eternal brother in Christ David Hound Blanton (1954-2018)

"Hound" a US Army Ranger who served in Vietnam joined the Patriot Guard Riders (PGR) in 2009 only a few years after its formation and maintained an unapologetic respectful determination to honor our nations heroes…. Through his years in PGR he routinely sacrificed time with his friends and family to ensure that old Glory had a flag holder at all corners of our land no matter the miles, the weather or whatever else may hinder the opportunity to show the honor and dignity that America's heroes deserved… all the way up until the day he took his last breath the mission of the Patriot Guard Riders was central to his very existence…at the time he departed this Earth he held the position of Georgia State Captain and he led with boots on the ground sometimes as a lone flag holder but more often leading the masses… his example has forever molded the character, determination and dignity of this honorable organization.

Don "BigDon" Wilson

Georgia State Captain

Patriot Guard Riders

www.PatriotGuard.org

AN INTRODUCTION TO THIS BOOK

Over the past several years, as I have written and published numerous Ride Reports following missions with the Patriot Guard Riders, more than once I've been told that I should compile these reports into a book. I've always been the self-deprecating type, and my first thoughts were, nobody would ever read it if I did. So, if you're reading this, congratulations.

In 2007 the Patriot Guard Riders had been in existence for almost two years, and yet I had never heard of them. I had a neighbor in the subdivision where I was living by the name of Stan Shaw. One day he was telling me about this motorcycle group that he had joined up with, how they went to the funerals of soldiers killed in action, in case anyone decided to disrupt the funeral, and how cool it was. I was in between motorcycles at the time, so it didn't really strike a chord with me, but I kept that thought in the back of my mind, and knew that when I got back on two wheels, I'd look these people up, see what they were all about, and join up with them.

In the meantime, my buddy Stan was down in Panama City Fl, riding his bike, no helmet on. He lost control of the bike somehow, and was killed in the ensuing accident. My wife and I went to the funeral home just outside Conyers for the visitation, and when we pulled up, here were all these biker types, some with long hair, beards, leather, standing outside the funeral home, holding American flags, and I thought, "how cool", only to find out upon leaving that they were members of the Patriot Guard Riders.

I told my wife, I have got to get another bike, I want to do 'cool' stuff like that, not realizing at the time that riding a motorcycle was not a requirement for membership, That the only requirement was respect for those who have sacrificed to preserve the freedoms that we enjoy.

It took a little persuading, but I finally talked her into it, and I became the proud owner of a 2004 Kawasaki Vulcan 750 (worst bike I have ever owned, by the way) and in August of 2008, I went online and joined the Patriot Guard Riders. I didn't attend my first mission until almost the end of September at a Funeral

Home in Snellville, and I would like to say that I remember the ladies name, but she and her husband were both members, and I believe she had died from cancer. I do remember that the Ride Captain for that mission was 'Nano', known to the regular world as Michael Louviere, and that his wife Elaine gave me some pointers of what we were supposed to do, as we stood in the flag line outside the funeral home.

A word of explanation; what we in the Patriot Guard call "standing the flag line" is probably the most common thing we do. We stand at the entrance to the Funeral Home, the Church, even individual homes, where ever we are needed, holding American flags as a show of respect for the person that we are there to honor. Visitors entering or leaving pass between the flags, and they are reminded that this person sacrificed on their behalf. It's not fun, it's not glamorous, we don't do it to get our picture in the paper or our face on television, we do it simply because "it's the right thing to do".

It has been my honor to stand the flag line with my Patriot Guard brothers and sisters in 7 different states, from Florida to New York, as well as participating in escorting remains in 9 different states. I've been on a boat going across Apalachicola bay, as we carried the remains of the mother of one of our members to a small island, where we had to remove boots, and roll pants up to disembark, so we could stand a flag line on this small island, where we held a short memorial service and her ashes were scattered.

I was at the National Cemetery in Saratoga, NY when the remains of an unknown Union Soldier were laid to rest in his native soil. I've held crying mothers, widows, and even grown men broken down in tears. I've shed more than a few tears of my own, which is why we wear dark glasses. I've heard probably every version of "Taps" that there is, and I can tell you that a live version beats a recorded one any day of the week, but either one will bring tears to my eyes.

I've had the pleasure of riding alongside of some of the finest men and women that I have ever met. Over the course of my service, I've had to say a final 'farewell' to some of them, and there go some more tears. I've stood at gravesides, where the entire cemetery was packed with people, and at gravesides where there were just a handful of folks, but the graves were exactly the same size. There's a lesson to be learned right there, one we would all do well to remember. When the Bible says "tomorrow is promised to no man", that's exactly what it means. Remember that.

I hope the following ride reports, covering almost 10 years of service with the Patriot Guard Riders of Georgia, gives you a little insight into what we do, and why we do it.

I have added pictures from my own collection, as well as some taken by our very own Gary "Photog" Adams, professional photographer and Patriot Guard Rider, as well as David "Hi-Tech Redneck" Andrews and several other PGR photographers.

It's all about Honor and Respect.

With Honor and Respect
Serving with the Patriot Guard Riders

CHAPTER ONE

I suppose, like any good story, you should start from the beginning, but where it actually began is somewhat hard to determine. The Patriot Guard Riders began in 2005 in Kansas, in response to a group of (to put it politely) misguided religious bigots from Topeka, who had taken their message of hate and divisiveness to the funerals of military members killed in Iraq and Afghanistan. They were disrupting these solemn occasions with vile signs and slogans that bore little resemblance to that portion of the Bible where Jesus said for us to "love your neighbor".

The Patriot Guard expanded to a nationwide organization, with approx. 100,000 members as best I can recall when I came on board. Now we count over 300,000 members and still growing, and the mission has grown as well. Along with the original mission of shielding the families of fallen Heroes from protesters, the Patriot Guard will, if requested, stand for any Active Duty Military personnel, as well as any honorably discharged veteran, law enforcement officer, fire fighter or other first responder. The key factor is, always, we have to be invited, we don't just show up, we're there as guests, the adore-mentioned protesters are uninvited guests, or ugs, as we like to call them.

The funerals of those who have been killed in action (KIA) always draw the largest response from our members, and non-members alike. They are also the funerals which attract the attention of the "uninvited" also. Just as a side note, girlfriend and I were in Clarkesville, TN around Thanksgiving 2010, visiting my sister and brother-in-law, as well as some of her family. While we were there, the Tennessee Patriot Guard was tasked with the mission of escorting a fallen soldier from Ft. Campbell, to a funeral home there in Clarkesville, so the gf and I thought we would join them for this escort. Enroute to the designated staging area, we passed a group of what looked to be Junior High students that were having a fund-raising car wash, however, the colored signs that they were holding alongside the road to promote this event were very close to the color of the signs used by the "uninvited"'

Once the fallen soldier's escort was underway, we once again passed these students, as we were heading to the funeral home. The escort arrived without incident; the casket was wheeled into the funeral home as honors were rendered. As the funeral home doors closed, and we all mingled about the parking lot, one man seemed particularly incensed, "Did you see them _____ (using the name for the "uninvited") people back there, holding up them signs! I wanted to get off my bike and whip their ass". At that point I felt compelled to tell him what was actually taking place back up the road, and I think he felt a little sheepish after that.

I have never personally laid eyes on any of the "uninvited". They learned pretty quickly that if they came to Georgia, the Patriot Guard Riders would make certain that they were not seen or heard, and that's not the way they like to operate, so good riddance to them. If you wish to protest against those who have given everything they had to give to protect your right to protest, there is certainly a better time and place for that, then at the funeral of that person who died for you. And there are much more effective ways of communicating your message. You claim to preach the gospel, but Jesus never taught his disciples to hate. You may not agree with the Global war on Terror, that's your right, but know this, that as long as you try to spread your hatred at the funerals of American Heroes, the Patriot Guard Riders will be there, exercising our rights as well, in a non-violent, non-confrontational way, to make sure that no family has to suffer the indignity of the "uninvited' Okay, rant over.

The first large KIA mission that I attended was in May of 2009, in Dallas, Ga. I had been in the Patriot Guard for almost a year, but holding down a full-time job had limited my ability to attend missions, and ten years later, I still find myself with the same challenge. I remember many things about this particular mission: motorcycles completely filled the parking lot of the funeral home (I believe that there were close to 200 bikes there) another thing that I will always remember, there was a television reporter looking for an interview, so naturally he was told to go to the State Captain, who was in attendance. They had to go get "Nano" out of the flag line, so the interviewer could talk to him. That made a huge impression on me, that the State Captain was standing the flag line, just like everyone else. We always say that the most important position in the Patriot Guard is "flag holder", and "Nano" exemplified that, and I've never forgotten it.

But the most meaningful thing I took away from this mission was the Ride Report filed by the Ride Captain in Charge, Bill Gaskins, as known as "RT". Bill was out of Savannah, but here he was, on the other side of the state, running a mission for a fallen Hero, because it was the right thing to do. His Ride Report was one of the most moving things I have ever read. To this day I cannot pick it up without tears coming to my eyes. In honor of Ryan Charles King, here is the Ride Report that "RT" wrote.

Specialist Ryan Charles King. Say the name quietly to yourself and commit it to memory.

Ryan wanted to be a soldier as early as ten years of age. I didn't know Ryan. I didn't know what his dreams and aspirations were. But I know he was a soldier and he stood in the gap between what I love about America and all who wish her harm. That gap is a lonely place sometimes and standing there is a huge burden to bear for a 22 year old Georgia boy. Knowing where SPC King was and what he was doing, I wonder if he knew...really knew...how much of a difference he was making in keeping this nation safe. On May 1, 2009 I would not imagine that thoughts of red, white and blue or apple pie or baseball were going through Ryan's mind. It was more likely his brother on his left and his other brother on his right. It was his wife and his family.

Ryan's journey home most likely took him through Bagram AF, near Kabul. No matter what time of the day or night, the base went quiet as the Humvee bearing SPC King and pallbearers made their way down Disney, past the Pat Tillman Center and onto the flightline. The streets were lined with Soldiers, Sailors, Airmen and Marines who stood silently as Ryan passed. Thousands of Ryan's brothers and sisters came to attention and rendered a final salute...many watched with eyes blurred by tears, not knowing Ryan's name but knowing a Brother-In-Arms had fallen. The flightline is normally loud and busy, but during the procession and ceremony to follow, it was silent. Ryan deserved no less.

We, the Patriot Guard Riders, became aware that Georgia had lost a son on Monday, May 4. With heavy hearts, we went about the task of planning an Honor Mission. There are so many people who made this mission work. The many people who were at the airport when SPC King arrived...thank you. You made a difference. Steve Sweat, who didn't hesitate for even a second when he was asked to be RCIC at the airport... thank you. ALR members, from Post 111 and others...thank you. Captain Williams, the CAO...thank you. You are a compassionate and professional officer. All of the Law Enforcement Agencies involved, thank you. Those who worked quietly behind the scenes to bring each detail together, thank you so much. The people of Paulding County...thank you so much. You spread the word and you showed a family you care. You are the faces of America. Our PGR members, new and not-so-new, thank you just doesn't suffice. All of those who had special passengers, thank you for carrying such precious cargo safely.

On Tuesday May 12, 2009 the Thunder rolled in Hiram/Dallas, Georgia. We came from every direction to make a small payment on a huge debt we owe to SPC Ryan King. Among us were Veterans, Warriors, Gold Star and Blue Star Mothers, young and not so young, in other words, a Grateful America. We came to pay our respects to Ryan. To show Ryan's family that their loss has not gone unnoticed. To stand in honor of Ryan and in support of his Brothers and Sisters still in the fight. To escort Ryan home. The most important thank-you goes to Ryan's family. Thank you for allowing us to come.

Instead of a chronological account of the day's events, I want to just mention some memories of the day. The streets and medians lined with American Flags Hundreds, maybe thousands of the King family's neighbors along the route, many with American Flags. Signs in front of churches and businesses in support of the King family. A UPS driver with a hastily made sign that said "thank you" Cars pulled to the shoulder of the road and drivers standing in respect for Ryan. Workers pausing to pay their respects as Ryan passed. Police and Fire Departments and EMS lining the route. I-75 northbound being shut down...completely... for Ryan An Honor Guard that was as perfect as I've ever seen. All of these things and so much more... Ryan C. King deserved no less.

When you remember the day, it's images, its emotions, don't stop there. Remember why we came to Paulding County. Remember that on May 1, 2009 in a dusty, rocky place seven thousand miles from home a young man from Paulding County, Georgia fought and died for his brothers and sisters, family and friends and for our freedom and safety. A gift like that cannot be forgotten.

Specialist Ryan Charles King. Say the name quietly to yourself and commit it to memory. He deserves no less.

When "RT" resigned from his position with the Patriot Guard Riders to pursue other endeavors, I wrote him a note to let him know what an impact this Ride Report had on me, and how much I appreciated his ability to put down on paper the events of that day. Many of our Ride Captains file reports that are one or two paragraphs, and that's fine, they cover all the facts, but I can put the blame squarely on "RT" for the fact that I have to get a little deeper into the mission than just the facts. When people read one of my ride reports, and tell me, "I felt like I was there" then it's a good report.

About mid-August that same year, I was looking thru the mission postings on the Patriot Guard's National website, and one particular mission caught my eye. "Unknown Union Soldier", being the history buff that I am, I almost came out of my seat. The remains of a Union soldier had been discovered on the battlefield at Sharpsburg, Md, also known as the Battle of Antietam. He was determined to be from the State of New York, by the buttons of his uniform, and his remains were being returned to New York for military burial, and the Patriot Guard Riders were going to escort his remains from Maryland to Saratoga New York.

Well, being a Civil War buff, and a former New Yorker, this was one PGR mission that I did not want to miss. I explained to my then wife (soon to be ex-wife #3) all the reasons why I had to go, but she wasn't buying any of it. So, of course, I made plans to go anyway.

Little did I know at the time that there were two other PGR riders who were also looking at that same mission. Ed Kornowski, from Buffalo, NY, and Dave (Dw) Taylor from Farmington MO, would play a part in this mission, and beyond, as we three became friends almost immediately, and that friendship continues to this day.

Unknown Union Soldier Mission

Antietam to Saratoga National Cemetery Sept 15 – 18, 2009.

Left Stockbridge Ga. this morning at 0605 and arrived in Martinsburg, WV at 1810, having covered 680 miles in almost exactly 12 hrs. Dave Taylor from Missouri and Ed Kornowski from Buffalo were already here, and had driven over to Antietam to check things out. Ed and I went to dinner at Hoss's steak house, great salad bar, and the steak was pretty good also. Back at the motel, it's after 9 pm. and I'm looking forward to tomorrow. Not really sure what to expect, but if this goes off like it might, it's going to be big, really big. So, we will see what tomorrow brings.

Sept. 25, 2009

Now that I have the opportunity to look back and reflect on this, the longest mission I've ever been on, or hope to be on, it was a most interesting experience, and one that I shall never forget. Tuesday dawned a beautiful day, although a bit cool. The three of us had breakfast at our motel, and then loaded up for the 20 something mile run up to Sharpsburg, Md. We arrived at the National Cemetery at Antietam around 8;20 pm and we were the first PGR people there. There were already a number of Park Service people, rangers and such already present, as well as some active-duty military, whose job seemed to be getting everything on camera, be it still or video. We got our flags, and placed ourselves in across from the chapel at the cemetery entrance, as that was where the transfer was to take place.

About that time, another group of bikes showed up, with 3 riders who had come down from NY. Just before 9 am, when the transfer ceremony was to take place, 2 more bikes showed up, with a Ride Captain from West Virginia, since it appeared that Maryland PGR was going to completely ignore this ceremony which was taking place in their back yard. The transfer itself was rather quick. A black SUV backed up to the cemetery gate, in the back was an unfinished pine coffin, made to the specifications of coffins from the Civil War era. The coffin was removed by Park Service Rangers, and carried into the chapel, and the doors closed. We later learned that the unknown soldiers remains were placed in the coffin at this point. Two members of the New York Honor Guard covered the coffin with a 34-star flag, and then it was once again carried out by the Park Service Rangers and placed in the back of the SUV.

At that point, we broke down the flag line, and scrambled for our bikes. By the time I got my flag put away, and my helmet on, I was the last bike to pull out, so I had the 'hearse' SUV directly behind me. We had LEO escort all the way to Interstate 81, and we took off across Maryland and into Pennsylvania. Somewhere in Pa, we picked up a group of about 15 bikes that was sitting on the side of the interstate waiting for us. We stopped for gas and lunch in Hamburg, Pa. around 11:15 am or so. Left there around noon, on thru PA and into New Jersey. There we stopped again, and picked up the NY PGR Riders, led by Ride Captain Bill Shaaf, who was a really cool guy. I tanked up with gas again, and we headed out, thru New Jersey and into New York. We changed routes several times, and as is usually my habit, I was paying much more attention to the bikes in front of me, then I was to the signs and roads that we were on. When you are running 75 to 80 mph like we were, you have to really keep a sharp eye on what is going on in front of you, cause if someone messes up, you have very little time to react.

So we're cruising along, 75 – 80 mph, on this four lane road, when my bike made a very bad sound, and started to slow down. I twisted the throttle, and could see the rpm gauge was still at 4800 rpms, but I was slowing down, and that was not good. Managed to get over to the side of the road, and up over the curb into the grass, without causing any wrecks, and coasted to a stop. To my dismay, the remainder of the bikes went right on by, and within a few seconds I was alone on the side of the road, with absolutely no idea where I was. Kind of a bad feeling.

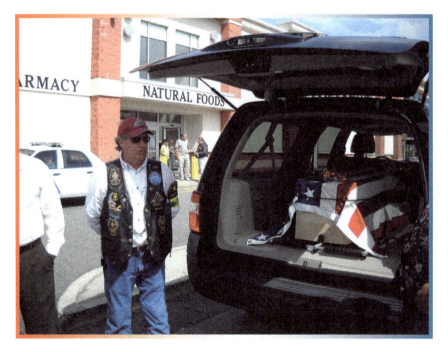

After cranking the bike up again, and determining that something between the engine and the back wheel was gone, I shut it down and called 911. They transferred me to the Thruway Authority, who wanted to know where I was at. Darn good question. All I could tell them was that I was at mile marker 26.3. That didn't seem to mean any more to them than it did to me. They wanted to know if I was in New York or New Jersey? I thought I was in New York, but couldn't swear to it. All I could say was that it was two lanes going North, and that there were a lot of cars going by like a bat out of hell, which didn't help much either, since that seems to be standard driving procedures for drivers in that area.

I tried calling Ed, and had to leave him a message, and right about this time, my cell phone battery went dead. Fortunately, I had the hospital cell phone, but I couldn't call Ed on it, because his number was only in my phone, and of course, he didn't have that number, so it was a total cluster. After over an hour of sitting on the side of the road, making calls back to the hospital trying to have someone locate a motorcycle repair shop in the area, which was really fun, since I didn't really know where I was, a H.E.L.P. operator showed up, and he called a tow truck to come get my bike. About the time the tow truck showed up, so did Ed, and another guy named Bob, who was a local, and knew of a shop where I could take the bike.

So, the tow truck driver loaded up the bike, and Ed met us over at the cycle shop, called Rockwell Cycles. We unloaded the bike, and I paid the tow truck drive $143 and change. Left the bike with Nick, the shop owner, and Ed rode me on the back of his bike up to Camp Smith, where the Unknown Soldier was lying at the chapel, with the Honor Guard in attendance. We paid our respects, and then went out looking for Orange County Choppers, which we finally found after getting bad directions twice. Took a couple of pictures, and then went and checked in at our motel, which was not the nicest place, but at that point I didn't really care. We unloaded our stuff, and ran down the street to a small pub to get something to eat.

Wednesday, September 16, was another beautiful day. I rode the back of Ed's bike up to Camp Smith, and we prepared to start out for Saratoga. Bill Shaaf was there and we had about 30 bikes when we started out. I got to ride in a 'cage' with a guy named Bob Kepler, who was a local, and one of the guys who had come down to Antietam on Tuesday. Real nice guy, PGR member from almost the start, Vietnam vet, all round nice guy. We had a great time riding together, found out that he was a born-again believer, but his wife was Catholic, and they went to a Catholic church. As we made our way north from Camp Smith, we seemed to add more bikes with every town we went thru. By the time we got to Albany, we probably had around 80 bikes, which made a pretty impressive sight, as we passed the state Capital.

Fast forward to the year 2019. This was as far as I got in writing the story of this Unknown Union Soldier mission, because it kind of had a bad ending for me personally, and although I've told the story countless times, I will now tell you, as Paul Harvey says, "the rest of the story".

Our escort arrived in Saratoga, NY, at the New York State Military Museum, around 4 pm on Sept. 16, 2009. The wooden casket, draped with the 34-star flag, was carried inside by six Civil War Reenactors in full period uniform. The casket was displayed prominently in the museum's rostrum, I suppose you could call it, flanked by an honor guard of one member of the Civil War Reenactors and one member of the New York State National Guard, in full dress uniform. The Patriot Guard stood a flag line at the entrance to the museum, until visiting hours ended at 8 pm, then Bill Shaaf lead the entire group into the museum to render honors en mass.

Ed and I went to eat, then back to our hotel. There were several other Patriot Guard guys there, most from New York, and they wanted to know how I was doing, had I found out anything about my bike, etc. At that point, I had not heard from the shop where it had been hauled to, and I told them that I'd worry about the bike when the mission was finished. That seemed to resonate with them, as I was to find out later.

September 17, 2009 dawned cloudy and cool, cool enough to wear a jacket, and I wasn't even riding a motorcycle. As best I can remember, we weren't scheduled to leave the Military Museum until around 10:30 am for the escort to Saratoga National Cemetery for an 11am burial service, so I had some free time that I spent mostly on the phone with the cycle shop, trying to find out what was wrong with my bike, and how long would it take to fix, and how much was it going to cost?

The Patriot Guard was staging at a large parking lot just down the hill from the Military Museum, and I made my way down there around 10 am, for the mission briefing. Bill Shaaf was giving the briefing, as he was the Ride Captain In Charge for this mission, I was standing off to the side, after all, I was hitching a ride in a cage (car, for those of you in Rio Linda) so I wasn't to attentive, until Bill called my name, asked me to step forward. He then proceeded to tell all those assembled about me riding my bike up from Georgia, and about my bike tearing up, and how I was determined to finish out the mission.

He than stuck the biggest wad of money I had ever seen in my hand, and told me that they had taken up a collection to help pay for the repairs to my bike. I am not ashamed to admit that tears were falling freely, and I tried to say "Thank you" and hopefully it came out in a way that folks present could understand the depths of the feelings that just overwhelmed me at the time.

Motorcycle people are some of the most generous in the world, and we have an expression of "Brothers taking care of brothers", and I certainly felt the brotherhood that cool morning in Saratoga, NY.

So, after hugging all the guys and girls that were there, and trying to tell them "thank you" individually, we trooped back up the hill, and rendered honors as the casket was carried out to the hearse by six Civil War Reenactors. The door closes, "mount up", and I go find Bob Kepler's car, and we're trailing the pack out to the cemetery.

Pulled into the cemetery entrance, and it was like "what the heck"? All the bikes were stopped because the cemetery was jammed with people. There were school buses parked on the side of the driveway, cars everywhere, it was amazing. TV camera trucks, reporters, everyone seemed to want to be a part of saying a final good-bye to this Unknown Soldier. Bob finally found a place to park, and we climbed out of the car, and started following the crowd over toward the shelter where the service was to take place.

Somewhere along the way, I go waylaid by a female TV reporter, who had somehow found out about my story, so I guess somewhere in Upstate NY, my ugly mug appeared on somebody's TV screen. Walked on down to the shelter as a horse drawn carriage rolls up, with the wooden coffin in the back, still covered with that 34-star flag. The Civil War Reenactors hoist it on their shoulders and carried it into the shelter, as the Patriot Guard rendered honors once again.

The service is conducted by a chaplain from the New York National Guard, and his remarks were followed up by a two-star General from the same outfit. The flag is folded by two members of the National Guard Honor Guard, and the Sgt in charge knelt and presented to a female reenactor, in a black period dress, representing either the wife or mother this Soldier left behind. Then the casket is carried to the grave side on the shoulders of the New York National Guard Honor Guard, led by the two-star General, and another reenactor, who was the spitting image of Ulysses S. Grant. It was quite a sight to behold.

Military honors are rendered again at the graveside. As the casket is laid down by the Honor Guard, the most unique 21-gun salute that I have ever seen is unfolding. The first volley of seven shots is fired by the Civil War Reenactors, the second volley is fired by the American Legion post from Schylerville, and the third volley is fired by the New York National Guard Honors team. The wooden casket is slowly lowered into the ground as those haunting notes of "taps" float over the assembled multitudes. One Hundred and Forty-Three years to the day, this son of New York finally rest in his native soil.

At his morning briefing, Bill Shaaf had announced that the American Legion post in Schylerville would be serving lunch for all the Patriot Guard Riders, so Bob and I hopped in his car and off we went. I called the cycle shop that had my bike, and they were wanting me to find the parts for them to fix it. I was a little taken back, I've never had that happen before.

Got to the Legion post in Schylerville, and they had an abundant feast laid out. Grilled sausage, hot dogs, potato salad, baked beans, rolls, it was an excellent feast.

The primary topic of conversation over lunch seemed to be my bike. One fellow told me of a cycle shop nearby that had a bike that was the same as mine, and they were going to work on the bike over the winter, and that I might be able to get the parts I needed from them. There were several other suggestions along those lines, and I appreciated everyone's concern. Then an angel stepped in, in the form of Jill Pellitier (I hope that is the correct spelling for her last name). She was attending her first PGR mission, and was listening to the conversations taking place regarding my bike. She knew I was from Georgia, and she said, "I've got some friends in Georgia that I haven't seen in a while. I have a truck and a trailer; I'll be glad to trailer your bike back to Georgia for you."

Wow, talk about speechless! You don't get an offer like that every day of the week. She gave me her card, this was on Thursday, noon, she said 'call me tomorrow if you haven't been able to get your bike fixed, I'll bring the truck and trailer and pick it up tomorrow evening, take you back to Georgia'. I took her card and thanked her profusely, but in the back of my mind I'm thinking, 'yeah right, lady, you're going to take some stranger that you just meet, and haul him and his bike a thousand miles to get him back home, yeah right'.

Bob and I headed back to toward his house, after telling everyone good-bye, and thanking them again for their generous donation. Bob Kepler was a wonderful soul, he told me, 'you come stay at my house for as long as you need'. And you could tell that he sincerely meant it. I was truly blessed on this trip, in so many ways. On the way back to Bob's house, we stopped by the shop that had been mentioned as having a bike like mine, and sure enough, there it was. Now all I had to do was convince them to sell me the rear drive assembly, and we were good to good. No dice. They were willing to sell me the whole bike, but not the parts that I needed off of it, so that prospect flew out the window in a hurry.

So, disappointed, we got back in the car, and headed south. Bob and lovely wife Lisa lived in Orange County, NY, home of the famous Orange County Choppers, and had a very nice home there. Bob was a handyman like myself, and he had to show me some of the projects that he had done around the house, I was quite impressed.

Friday morning, Bob and Lisa both had things to do, so I had the house to myself. I used Bob's computer to try to locate the parts I needed for the bike, as well as talking to the shop that had the bike, and they're still fussing about me finding the parts. I had also phoned the wife in Georgia at the time the bike broke down, and told her 'we have a problem', her exact response, and I've never forgotten it was, "We don't have a problem, you have a problem. You got yourself into this, you get yourself out the best way you know how". It just warmed my heart to hear such loving words coming from the person who is supposed to be your life partner. And further along is the same conversation, she was kind enough to tell me that I could fly back to Georgia and just leave the bike there. That was not a viable option in my view, so there I was.

Picked up her card and called Jill Pellitier, thinking all the time that she was going to have some reason for now following thru on what she had promised me yesterday at the Legion hall in Schylerville, but she was true to her word. She said she had to drop a friend off at the airport around 2 pm, and then she'd go back home, hitch up the trailer to the truck. I gave her Bob's address, and she said 'I'll see you around 6 pm'. Praise the Lord! Called the cycle shop that had my bike, told them we would be there around 6:30 to pick up the bike. The guy said, 'we close at 6', I told him to set the bike outside, in that case, I don't think anyone is going to steal it.

Jill showed up at Bob's house about 6:30 pm, truck, trailer, and her brother along riding shotgun. I said good-bye to Bob and Lisa, thanked them so much for their generous hospitality, threw my stuff in the back of the truck, and off we went to the cycle shop. Got there just before 7 pm, and the manager was still waiting, although he was not happy about it, and didn't make any pretense of hiding that fact. Paid him $180 for tearing the bike apart to find out what was wrong with it, got it loaded up, and we headed south. Stopped for fuel somewhere in New Jersey around 10 pm. Stopped again in Virginia sometime in the early morning. Got fuel in South Carolina sometime after daybreak, and around 2 pm on Saturday, September 19, Jill backed the trailer up to my garage, and we unloaded the bike. Mission complete.

Jill and her brother had just one request at that point, they wanted to take a shower before leaving out, and I was glad to accommodate. My soon to be ex-wife had arrived along with her sister, while we were unloading the bike, and she certainly did not look glad to see me, wouldn't even get out of the car to say hello to Jill and her brother. Oh well.

To finish up the story, on Monday, I called Rockdale Cycle in Conyers, Ga, about a 30-minute drive from my house. Yes, they had the rear drive assembly that I needed. Picked it up, borrowed a trailer from a friend of mine, loaded up the bike and took it to my mechanic and dropped it off. Headed back to my friend's house to return the trailer, I saw a guy with a motorcycle broke down on the side of the road. I pulled over, we loaded his bike on the trailer, and I took him to his mechanic in Stockbridge, and had to tell him the story of the lady who trailered my bike back from NY. So, I got to pay it forward, a little bit.

Wednesday, my mechanic called, "she's ready to go". Thanks to the generous donations from the PGR in New York, I still had about $60 left over, when it was all said and done, and paid for.

As has been noted before, motorcycle people are some of the most generous in the world. They do charity rides, almost year-round in Georgia. In the fall they raise money for organizations like Wreaths Across America, and as it gets closer to Christmas, you'll find them doing toy runs for those kids who would not have a Christmas otherwise. And if your motorcycle breaks down a thousand miles from home, somebody might just step up and offer to trailer it home for you.

New York Ride Captain Bill Shaaf had apparently been taking lessons from "RT" because his ride report was almost five pages long, but it was a good one.

This recap may get distorted by our e-mail master lister. I have included this recap as a word document. Be sure to see the most recent video release by the New York State Department of Military and Naval Affairs – link at the end of the report.

It's has now been two weeks since the Patriot Guard participated in what was one of the most impactful Missions that we shall ever see. Over three days the PGR was there to escort home to New York a Union Soldier who lost his life on the Antietam battlefield on September 17, 1862 – A Soldier Known But To God.

These last 14 days I've had my regular job to do as well as being a part of three other PGR missions but I didn't want another day to go by without remarking on this wonderful experience.

This mission actually started some 5 months ago when I learned that Saratoga National Cemetery would most likely have a Civil War soldier to bury sometime this year. I thought to myself – if ever there was a Patriot Guard Riders mission to be a part of, this would be it. I broke a cardinal rule of the PGR – we don't "mission shop" – we don't request of others Patriot Guard Rider involvement in a funeral, we must be asked.

I started to make inquires to learn more about the Civil War soldier slated to come home to New York. I met with Mike Aikey, the Director of the Saratoga Military Museum, who in turn directed me to Don Roy, Director of the Military Services Honor Guard. I introduced myself and explained who we were (PGR) and asked if they would consider having the PGR provide an escort from Antietam.

It wasn't as much of a long shot as I had thought - Don Roy was in charge of bringing the soldier home to New York and I saw a picture of his Harley behind the desk. I was honored that he invited me to be a part of the planning for this ceremony.

We waited a long time for the Smithsonian and/or the Antietam National Battlefield Park professionals to tell us something about whether we were ever going to get this soldier home. Late in August we got word to come and get our soldier. Don Roy made the right call when he said the Honor Guard would be there to pick our soldier up at Antietam on Tuesday, 9/15 so that we could honor him with a burial in Saratoga National Cemetery on Thursday, 9/17 – 147 years to the day he was killed in Millers Cornfield.

A planning meeting came together quickly, with representatives of the Military Honor Guard and their Public Relations people along with representatives of the Civil War Re-enactors, Saratoga Military Museum, Saratoga National Cemetery Director and staff and I representing the PGR.

This was a brainstorming session about how to put all the various puzzle parts together for this ceremony. I was fortunate to have funeral home clients that could provide the horse drawn carriage, the bagpipe and drum band and a hearse.

The whole mission started to come together pretty smoothly (although I didn't know I had the horses for the carriage until we were leaving Camp Smith on Wednesday morning – not going to bore you with why its difficult to get horses in Saratoga but it has to do with bagpipes and 21 gun salutes).

One little wrinkle did occur. The Honor Guard was just going to be part of a small, respectful transfer ceremony down in Antietam. As the word got out many PGR members were telling me they were going to Antietam for the ceremony – hadn't planned on this and finally the Maryland PGR was able to get a Ride Captain over there to RC this part.

Although I wasn't present at the transfer ceremony in Antietam National Battlefield, from the videos I have seen and from talking to those that were there, it was obvious that the staff at the Park were profoundly moved by what was taking place. In some way, shape or form, Antietam National Battlefield, that place, had been the custodian of this soldier for 147 years. Once discovered, the Antietam National Battlefield Park staff, led by Park Superintendent John Howard, was diligent in their care of the remains. They carried out a very dignified, honorable and respectful transfer to the New York Military Forces Honor Guard. Although the staff at Antietam fully supported the return of this soldier, this was personal to them - it's not hard to believe that there's a little hole in their hearts.

I can't say enough about how well law enforcement agencies stepped up for us. I made over 25 calls to all the appropriate police agencies from Antietam to Saratoga Springs. Once I told them who we were and what the mission was about they couldn't have been more supportive. For some police communities it was all hands on deck – it was really impressive to see, in community after community, as we made our way home, the blinking red, white and blue police lights escorting us along and making sure we got thru all the traffic. Hats off to them (which reminds me I have about 25 letters to write).

On Tuesday the PGR escort out of Antietam started off with 8 motorcycles. By the time the escort hit our staging area in Haskell NJ the escort had grown to 25. When we left Haskell we had over 50 bikes for the trip to Camp Smith where our soldier would lay in state overnight at Father Duffy Chapel.

Wednesday morning our long escort up Rt-9 to Saratoga Springs began with about 25 motorcycles. More and more bikes joined the procession as we traveled up Rt-9. About 40 bikes entered the staging area in Hudson, New York, were we met up with PGR and others that came down to join us. As we rolled thru downtown Albany on our way to Saratoga Springs we were 90+ strong - ¾ of a mile long.

I should mention that at all the staging areas and fuel stops along the way, Don Roy opened up the back of his escort vehicle to display for the public the 34 star flag draped coffin that had been prepared in Antietam with a wonderful garland ribbon around flowers – the ribbon's words "Known But To God"

Thursday, Sept 17, our escort from the museum to Saratoga National Cemetery again was 90+ motorcycles. I've been told that the 500 or so people waiting for us at the cemetery became stone cold silent when our motorcycles rumbled into the cemetery signaling the arrival of our soldier.

The procession of Civil War Re-enactor Honor Guards, US Military Honor Guards, bagpipers and drums playing "Going Home" and then the beautiful horse drawn carriage with the flag draped coffin inside was as awe inspiring a sight as I have ever seen. The whole ceremony at the cemetery, from start to finish, was emotional, professional, dignified, respectful, precise and done with great care and affection.

Some treasured memories:

- Seeing the riders from the others states join in our mission, especially the contingent that joined the escort at the PA/NJ border. Thanks to State Captain Bill "Hawk" Connelly for helping with this.

- Being at Camp Smith, early in the morning, alone with the soldier and your thoughts.

- Dave Taylor came to Antietam from Missouri –was to also to make the trip from Antietam to Saratoga but near Hershey, PA his cell phone summons him home on important business. He's home safe with wonderful memories of what happened at Antietam Battlefield that morning.

- Another PGR member came all the way from Georgia. Dave Shreckengost made it to Antietam and then onto New York. His bike transmission shredded on him just into New York.. Ed Kornowski, who made the trip from Buffalo, rode back to get Dave and brought Dave up to Camp Smith. Bob Kepler and friend were "caging" it from Peekskill with the escort and stayed thru the ceremonies at Saratoga National. Dave Shreckengost was able to ride up with Bob and then return to Peekskill later to see about his bike repairs – which were costly. At the briefing on Thursday morning, at the suggestion of PGR member Scott Smoke, we took up a number of collections for Dave and I think we were able to pretty much make a big dent in his repair problem. Dave was blown away and just couldn't thank us enough. Motorcycle brothers taking care of another brother – outstanding.

- As the escort moved up Rt-9 in the Hudson Valley; seeing how some communities turned out to show their respect. School children by the side of the road waving flags. Military and police contingents lined up and saluting. An American Legion Post lining both sides of the road – a bugler in the middle of the road playing taps while they fired a 21 gun salute. Some people with tears in their eyes for the return of this young soldier.

- Seeing and hearing the rumble of motorcycles as we made our way thru Saratoga Springs to the Military Museum and seeing hundreds of people lined up there to witness the transfer of our soldier to the museum where he was to lay in state for the rest of the day. The bagpiper playing as that transfer happened (15 yr old Michael Miller Jr.)

- Best seat in the house – looking in my mirrors and seeing a string of motorcycle headlights for as far back as I could see – pretty impressive.

- Just inside the entrance to the cemetery the procession was halted for a bit before we proceeded. Paul Lyman, on staff with the cemetery, met me and the first thing I asked was "Please tell me we have horses and a carriage" He said "Oh yeah – we got big horses and wait until you see the people that are here – this is huge". How right he was

- Getting to meet and speak with Karen L. Orrence, an archeologist with the National Park Service. Not just any archeologist but one of two that were involved in the excavation and examination of the soldiers remains. By her own admission she had "bonded" with the soldier and had come to Saratoga to see how and where he was to be buried. Karen had her "closure".

- Being with "bikers" with colors and leathers, many of them with watery eyes and when they did try to speak, a few words barely got out before many had to stop and re-compose themselves.

Some people to thank for making this all happen:

Don Roy, Director Military Forces Honor Guard, Latham, New York. Don was the guy who was responsible for making all this happen. It was Don Roy who allowed the Patriot Guard Riders to not only participate but have a hand in some of the planning for these ceremonies. donald.roy1@us.army.mil.

Mike DeMarco, DeMarco-Stone Funeral Home, Schenectady, New York. Mike was pleased to be able to provide his beautiful horse drawn carriage for the soldier's final trip.
demarco-stone@nycap.rr.com

Michael Miller and his son, Mike Jr (literally a World Class Piper), Brewer Funeral Home, Lake Luzerne, NY for getting members of his pipe band, Galloway Gaelic of Glens Falls to come and march and play – what a soundtrack for these ceremonies.
brewermillerfuneralhomes@yahoo.com

Joseph Turcotte, Flynn Brothers Funeral Home, Schuylerville, NY – for providing his hearse that was used from the Museum on Wednesday morning over to the cemetery then transfer to the horse drawn carriage.
joeflynnbros@verizon.net

Parker Brothers Funeral Home, Watervliet, NY. They provided the Civil War era pine box casket that was used to inter our Civil War Soldier.
MReinfurt@aol.com

Ernie Bessette, Teamster from Ft Edward, NY. Last minute hero who stepped up big time in getting those beautiful draft horses for the pulling of the carriage. Ernie validated his reputation as a top notch driver as he handled those big horses beautifully. (Ernie one time drove a team from Ft. Edward out to California).
wagonmaster1x@yahoo.com

I have included their e-mail addresses so that some might want to send them a note and tell them how you feel about what they did. I know all of them and they're great people.

A big thank you goes out to the American Legion Post # 278 in Schuylerville for hosting a very nice luncheon for all those who participated in the ceremonies on Thursday. They got there early and stayed well into the day to make sure we were fed and nourished.

Last but not least, I also wish to thank all of the Patriot Guard Riders and members of the other motorcycle clubs (Rolling Thunder, American Legion Riders, Combat Vets, Leathernecks MC and others) that participated over the three days. Your participation, presence and dignity made an impact on all of those who were witness to what we did. Special thanks go out to PGR NYS Ride Captains who were a great help along the way. John Tibbs – Senior Ride Captain for Region 7 and who took care of the staging location in Haskell, NJ. Region 6 Senior Ride Captain Ray McCarthy and his RC Brian Terralavoro (who "helped" LEO's during escort). Region 4 Senior Ride Captain Ken "PK" Hedden, Sr who managed the staging area in Hudson, NY and brought about 50 bikes down with him – along with his RC's Big Dan Nolin, Jack "Rabbit" Demers and Rick "Rickster" Moore. It's a comforting feeling to know I have these people to put my faith and trust in.

I have again included the link that was put together by a group called the Gathering of Eagles. This link contains some beautiful videos and links to other articles and pictures of the three day event.
http://nygoe.wordpress.com/2009/09/18/civil-war-soldier-returns-to-new-york/

I want to thank all of the PGR members who have sent me CD's/DVD's of pictures and videos of these ceremonies. Some day soon I'll get them in order and see about getting them posted on a site where we can all have access – they're wonderful.

NEW RELEASE: The New York State Department of Military and Naval Affairs have just released their video – you can see it here:
http://dmna.ny.gov/video/?v=Civil%2520War%2520Vet%2520Returns%2520Home%2520After%2520147%2520Years&assoc=

I have included this next link – from the movie Glory – it begins with the Battle at Antietam. It's a very sobering look at just what our young soldier must have experienced prior to his death on that battlefield…………it's difficult to imagine the horror.
http://www.youtube.com/watch?v=jeE-EMfH-kQ&feature=player_embedded

If I have failed to acknowledge anyone, it's certainly not intentional but a function old age and a bad memory.

I am proud & honored to be associated with such fine men and women as that of the Patriot Guard Riders. Those that were there for these ceremonies experienced something we may never see again in our lifetimes. May God bless us and keep us safe.

One final thought – something that I feel sums up most of our feelings those three days.

At the Museum, one of our PGR riders witnessed a very young Cub Scout who approached and touched the coffin and said, **"It's OK, you're home now. You don't have to be scared anymore"**.

Bill Schaaf
Patriot Guard Riders - Senior Ride Captain - Region 5
MIAP/VRP Coordinator Regions 4,5,6,7
V.P. PGRNY Board of Directors
billschaaf@aol.com
518-542-0608

With Honor and Respect

CHAPTER TWO

THE 'TEMPORARY' RIDE CAPTAIN

In the fall of 2009, Patriot Guard Mission requests went out to everyone who was in a leadership position, and whoever is a
up the mission. I had joined that select group, although technically at the bottom of the pile, having recently been promote
of mentor with the Patriot Guard Riders. Mentors are sort of an apprenticeship position, we are asked to 'mentor' new peopl
brief them on how to conduct themselves during a mission, etc., etc. When a mission request goes out, and no Ride Capt
mentors are encouraged to step up and handle the mission as 'temporary Ride Captains", as this is how you get experien
position I found myself in early in October, 2009.

RIDE REPORT – RUSSELL CAULEY, 10/02/2009

Sunday, October 4, 2009

Ride Report for the escort of retired Air Force veteran Russell Cauley. October 2,

There is an old saying, " Be careful what you wish for, you might get it ". That was somewhat the way I was feelin
October 1, as I was trying to pull together a very short notice mission to escort a retired Air Force veteran to his final
Canton National Cemetery. With less than 24 hrs. to the schedule departure from Clark Funeral Home in Hiram, it to
help of Lou (soretoe), and Larry Klein (eagle1) to get everything in order, or so I hoped.

After talking to Russell's sister, Patsy Whitlock, I learned that Russell was an avid motorcycle rider, and according to
his Harley's", and that two of Russell's Harley Davidson motorcycles were going to accompany him to Canton.

Friday, October 2, 2009 was still dark and overcast as I rolled out of Stockbridge and hooked up with Eagle 1 for the ride over to Hiram. Acting as the Temporary Ride Captain had given me a whole new perspective on what our Ride Captains do day in and day out, and I tried not to show how nervous I really was. This was a very short notice mission, and on a workday as well, and I was just hoping we would have enough bikes to cover the hearse. Knowing how well the members of the Ga PGR respond to these situations, I should have known better. When Eagle1 and I arrived at the funeral home, Soretoe was already there with flags, and several bikes.

As staging time of 9 am got closer, bikes continued to drift in, some singly, some in pairs, or three, until we had to start another line to accommodate them. Our original information from the funeral home had been that the funeral procession was going to depart at 10:30 am, but after arriving, and getting updated, I discovered that the departure had been changed to 10 am. Fortunately, there was already a good quantity of motorcycles sitting in the parking lot, so I felt like we were in good shape. At approx. 9:40 am, I conducted a ride briefing, aided by a 'cheat sheet' from Soretoe, because I was so nervous, I wasn't sure of my own name. But with the help of Eagle1 and Mark (Son-in-law) Taylor, I had managed to cover most of the points, when Eagle1 called the Patriot Guard to attention, as the funeral home had rolled the flag-draped casket out to the hearse without any prior notice. We remained at "Order Arms" until the casket had been loaded into the hearse, and wrapping the briefing up quickly, we mounted up and prepared to roll out.

The funeral procession rolled out a few minutes after 10 am, led by Russell's brother Ron, riding one of Russell's Harley's, and Russell's brother in law, Lynn Whitlock, and Russell's sister Patsy, on their own Harley, directly in front of the hearse carrying their brother to his final resting place. Because there had been no flag line at the funeral service on Thursday evening, the decision was made to place all of the PGR bikes between the hearse and the family vehicles, so that the family could get to see the line of flags that was accompanying this retired airman to Canton. Law Enforcement escort by the Paulding County Sheriff's office was flawless, ably assisted by two motorcycle escorts, and we moved thru Paulding County and out to I-75 with no problems whatever. North on I-75, to the Canton exit, where local law enforcement guided us securely to Canton National Cemetery.

Upon arrival at Canton, after a brief dismount at the reception area, we took all the motorcycles down to the shelter, where Soretoe was waiting with the flags, and a flag line was set up and in place when the hearse and family arrived at the shelter for the final committal service. After a few short, but very fitting remarks on the part of the minister, the flag was folded while taps were played, and the flag was presented to Russell's widow. Soretoe had a flag folded which had been flown on several PGR missions, which he gave to me, I had the honor of presenting it to Russell's mother. The entire family expressed their gratitude, time and time again, for the presence of the Patriot Guard. The entire family was absolutely in awe of the number of bikes that showed up, and once again, simply by being there, the Patriot Guard helped to soothe the hurt and to some extent, ease the pain of a suffering family, simply by doing what we do. Showing up, and letting them know that they are not alone, we care, and we are there for them.

Simple acts, that for most of us, if we were asked, would just say, "it's no big deal", to this family it was a very big deal, and we will never know this side of eternity the impact that the Patriot Guard had on this day, in this town, for this family.

PGR - PART OF IT, PROUD OF IT.

Toward the end of February, 2010, this mentor once again stepped up to take charge as 'temporary Ride Captain' for another mission.

Ride Report, Larry Thomas Dowdy, February 27, 2010

On a beautiful Georgia winter day, one that began with temperatures at or below freezing, and ended with sunshine and shirtsleeves, the Patriot Guard showed up in force at a small, rural Baptist church, and left an indelible impression on the family of Vietnam veteran Larry Dowdy. It was a short notice mission, with a temporary ride captain, but to the men and women of the Patriot Guard, it was an opportunity to once again stand up for someone who had stood up for them, and stand they did.

Larry Dowdy came from a family that knew what it meant to serve their country. There were four boys in the Dowdy family, and they all served in the military. Larry's brother John, said that between the four of them, they had almost 50 years of service. Larry's brother Mitchell was killed in Vietnam in 1972. Larry himself was injured during his service, when his ship caught fire, and he got trapped below decks while trying to extinguish the fire. Larry knew what it meant to serve, and Larry served his country to the best of his ability.

There are few things in life as beautiful as a line of flags, gleaming in the sun, and on Saturday, February 27, 2010, there were almost 40 of them, in line, and waving brightly, as Larry's widow, Shelia, and their children, some of whom Larry and Shelia had adopted, pulled into the parking area. As friends and well-wishers continued to stream in, again and again, they stopped to look in awe and wonder at the 'bikers' that had come to pay their respects to Larry.

To say "Thank you" to all those who made this mission possible, would not seem adequate to express my gratitude for all those who took part. The biggest "Thank You" of all has to go to the wonderful men and women who rode into the heartland of Georgia from all parts of the state, stood and honored Larry Dowdy without asking for any recognition or acclaim, and then rode away to their respective homes, carrying only the satisfaction of a job well done, it is you who make all of this possible, and from the bottom of my heart, "Thank You". You were awesome and made a difference, for one family, on one day, in a small Georgia town.

Those whose names I can remember, include State Captain Jeff (Jay Dub) Goddiel, who provided calm steadying guidance to a very nervous temporary RC. Lou (Soretoe) Costello who was not there, but was instrumental, along with Pam (keeper of peace) Long, in making sure that we had flags for visitation, which were brought over by George and Deddlebug. Bill Clark who brought flags and riders up from Augusta, to provide flags for Saturday. Big Rogg was up at 4 am on Saturday, putting the finishing touches on a condolence book that was absolutely beautiful, and then drove it down to Jefferson, Ga from his home up near Chattanooga.

Ride Captain Larry (Laru) Klein, who rolled in just in time to organize the flag line while the temporary ride captain went with Doug and Tobie Haynie and Jay Dub to escort the family. Doug Haynie, not only rode escort for Larry's family, but also presented the condolence book to Larry's widow Shelia. Keith (KP) Cheeks, Ga Mentor team, who welcomed two new members. Police Chief Randy Williams, of the City of Arcade, along with several of his officers, provided LEO escort, aided by deputies from Oconee County. It truly was a team effort, and one that truly was a beautiful sight to behold, at a small rural Baptist church, on a beautiful Georgia winter day.

As a 'temporary Ride Captain' I always hated it when "real" Ride Captains showed up at your mission, my thought was, "if you were available, why didn't you take the mission"? As a mentor, being very new to the organization, having "real" Ride Captains show up always made you very nervous, and very afraid you're going to make a mistake and look foolish. Fortunately, this didn't happen, and once I got promoted to "real" Ride Captain, I had the pleasure of dropping in on more than a mentor who was acting as 'temporary' Ride Captain on more than one occasion. Get to make them a little nervous, lol.

Probably one of the more unusual missions was the one you are about to read about, in that it all took place inside the Atlanta Renaissance Hotel at the Atlanta airport. We lined up on the stairwell that led to the Grand Ballroom, where a "Celebration of Life" took place.

Ride Report, Stan 'Bobby' Norton March 20, 2010

In doing missions for the Patriot Guard, there are a number of moments that make up the picture of a mission, a collection of small incidents that weave themselves together to make the whole thing come together, and this mission was no exception.

From the moment the request went out, this was going to be a unique mission. Stan's wife, Susan, told me that Stan didn't want anyone to cry for him, he wanted them to throw a party, and that is just was Susan was going to do, and she wanted the PGR to be a part of it. "A Celebration of Life" she called it, and that's just what it was.

There was that moment, when, 20 bikes strong, with flags flowing in a beautiful March afternoon in Georgia, the Patriot Guard roared up in front of the Renaissance Concourse Hotel to do their part in celebrating the life of Stan Norton.

The flag line, that cascaded in red, white, and blue down the staircase, and the moment when Susan and her daughter descended the stairs while 26 Patriot Guard members saluted.

There was the moment, at a table filled with pictures and memorabilia, that told of a life well lived, of good times, and motorcycles, and his Marine platoon, discharge papers, the stuff that life is made of.

The moment, when in the midst of celebration, you get called aside, and find out we have been asked to salute another fallen Marine at 8 am tomorrow, and the forecast is for rain.

The moments of an elderly minister, who had married Stan and Susan 25 yrs. earlier, now bringing words of comfort to those who were still feeling the loss.

The moment when our own Nick Petty (ancient 1) took the podium and told all those in attendance about Stan, and his service in the Marines, and to his country. Nick's speech fell on receptive ears, and he left the podium to a standing ovation, then lead the remaining members of the Patriot Guard out of the ballroom as the standing ovation continued.

The moment of saying good-bye to your fellow riders, " Be safe"," See you next time", and then off they go, and for a moment, you wonder if you really will. Then you push the start button, and move forward into another moment, knowing that for a moment, you made a difference for one family, in one moment in their lives.

Thank you's to Lou and JR, Mack, Nick, and to Trace, age 5, who got what we hope is the first of many

"Mission Complete" pins.

Sincerely

David Shreckengost (wild1handy)

Temporary Ride Captain, Patriot Guard Riders

Holding down a full-time job often meant that there were often long stretches in between missions where you served as 'temporary Ride Captain'. It was a rare exception that there were no Ride Captains available, and 'mentors' were allowed to step up and take a mission. But every time I got the opportunity, I would volunteer to take one, and each one had its own challenges and rewards.

Ride Report- Mitchell L. 'Mitch' Brown, July 7, 2010

It was one of those missions where you truly do not know what to expect. The Patriot Guard had been asked to stand for Army veteran 'Mitch' Brown, and that's all we were asked to do. When I originally contacted Margie Brown, Mitch's widow, she wanted us to stand a flag line prior to the 11 am Memorial Service. When I asked her what time, she would like us to be there, she said that she thought 10:45 would be fine. I told her we could do better than that, and that we would be there at 10 am.

After running out to Douglasville to pick up some flags from Soretoe, on the previous evening, I arrived at the funeral home in Peachtree City about 20 min early and did not see another soul. After introducing myself to the funeral director and receiving carte blanche to do whatever we wanted to do. I walked outside to see the very welcome sight of Big Harve and Big Rogg. Harve and I grabbed some flags and some stakes and we planted flags at the funeral home entrance, and along to drive opposite the entrance. By this time, we had been joined by 'Duck', who rode up from Columbus, Terry rode in on her red trike, and my own Elizabeth also joined us, and our flag line formed just as the family was arriving.

Just as the family walked up, Mitch's 92 Harley-Davidson Ultra Classic pulled up in front, driven by Mitch's best friend. The bike was parked, and Mitch's helmet was placed on the driver's seat, and his wife Margie's was placed on the passenger seat. Margie paused as she walked up, staring at the bike that she and Mitch had enjoyed for so many years. As she wiped the tears from her eyes, and walked thru the flag line, all she could say was "Thank you".

It was a refrain that we heard again and again, as Mitch's friends filed in to say good-bye to their friend, riding buddy, and fishing partner. The visitors streamed in steadily throughout the morning, as the sun got hotter and hotter. One by one, all the Patriot Guard members went inside to pay their respects. I went last, and Margie gave me a big hug, and said, "Mitch would have been so proud. Thank you for being here". It's difficult to tell, sometimes, what the impact of our mission's is, but on a hot July day, in Peachtree City, Ga. there was no doubt that the small presence of the Patriot Guard had a big impact on one family.

All missions are a compilation of numerous individuals, and this one was no exception. My hat is off to Big Harve, and Big Rogg, who drove down from Tunnel Hill, 'Duck', who made the trip up from Columbus, Terry from Griffin, Elizabeth postponed a Dr's appt to be there, and our own Lou Costello, who provided the flags, that looked so beautiful in the summer sun.

A job well done; mission completed.

Sincerely

David Shreckengost (wild1)

Temporary Ride Captain

Temporary Ride Captains don't normally get this type of mission. A young man, Active Duty United States Army had been killed tragically, and as best I can remember, Larry (Laru) Klein came down sick, and decided to give this mission to me. It was good experience for this temporary Ride Captain.

Ride Report, Sp4 Jonathan Michael McDonald 072410

There are some missions you plan for, and then some get handed to you without warning, and this mission falls in the latter category. When Larry (Laru) Klein called me on Friday night and asked me if I could take his mission on Saturday, it was one of those things you can't say no to. A fine young American had been tragically killed in an automobile accident in the prime of his life, and it was our job to see that he got the respect he deserved.

Fortunately, there were already flags in place at the Harvesttime Apostolic Ministries Church in Riverdale, so that was one item out of the way. When I arrived, I was the first PGR member there, which was also a first for me, and I couldn't help but wonder if it was a bad sign. But not to worry, this is Georgia, and the PGR always seems to show up in just the right numbers. By the time I got four flags planted along Hwy 85 in front of the church, Dorothy (from Texas, not Kansas) had arrived to stand with us. JR and Patti were the next to pull in, and I was glad to see them, it always helps to have an experienced ride captain along to make sure you haven't forgotten anything. Bikes continued to pull in until we had nine lined up, and two cages, for a total of 13 flag holders.

The hearse carrying Jonathan arrived shortly after 12, and PGR members were honored to assist in removing the casket and placing it on a gurney, to be rolled into the church. It was a tribute to the standing that Jonathan had in his community, people were filing into the church before we could conduct a proper briefing, so most of our briefing took place while our flag line was in place. We had one new member, Gary, who had ridden up from Columbus with Sparky and another rider. We stood the flag line for almost an hour before the arrival of the family, when we expanded our line to take in all four limousines, and surround this grieving family with the red white and blue.

We stood down after the service got underway, and after consulting with the funeral director, and JR, the decision was made to only have JR's and two other bikes in the funeral procession, due to the fact that Jonathan was being carried back to the funeral home in a horse-drawn hearse, and there were concerns over the Harley's overheating in this weather. But everything went off without a hitch, and Jonathan arrived safely back at the funeral home, with JR and Sparky, and another rider leading the family limousines. They were a beautiful sight to see.

The PGR again assisted in removing Jonathan from the horse-drawn hearse, and we presented arms and gave him our final salute, as he was wheeled back into the funeral home. His remains will be transported to Arlington National Cemetery, and he will be laid to rest there on July 30.

With every mission that we do, there are always moments that you will remember, and this one was no exception. After the hearse had arrived carrying Jonathan, the funeral home van arrived with the flowers, and some mementos of Jonathan. PGR members immediately sprang into action, carrying flowers and pictures into the church. I turned around and looked thru the glass entrance doors, to see JR, down on one knee, with Patti right over his shoulder, setting Jonathan's boots on a small stand, and hanging his dog tags on a rifle that was muzzle down.

They were taking such care to make sure that everything was just perfect, it captured in that one moment, the spirit of what we do. We take time off from our 'regular' lives, we ride, sometimes for many miles, to stand in any kind of weather, for people that most of us have never met, so that the families of these soldiers and veterans will know that we are there, and we appreciate the service of their son, brother, sister, uncle, father, mother, aunt. That their sacrifice has not one unnoticed, and JR and Patti demonstrated that commitment in their actions, those few minutes spent on their knees in the lobby of a church they'd never seen before, far better than I can put into words, if I wrote a thousand pages.

Respectfully submitted

David Shreckengost (wild1)

Temporary Ride Captain

Ga. Patriot Guard Riders

Some missions are long, covering two, three days, sometimes longer. Some are relatively brief, this one fell into the latter category, but still was a very moving mission

Ride Report- William Davis- USAF- Ga National Cemetery, 072610

On a steaming hot July Monday, I found myself once again on the hallowed ground of the Georgia National Cemetery in Canton, Ga. The Patriot Guard was coming to say their final farewells to William Davis. It had been a late post on the mission thread, and I wasn't sure what the response was going to be. As you turn off of Ga Hwy 20, and enter the cemetery grounds, you can't help but be impressed with the beauty of that piece of ground, and call to memory previous visits, to say farewell to others who served their country.

I found two bikes sitting in front of the reception area, and knew that we were off to a good start. Bikes and cages continued to arrive steadily, until there were 11 bikes and 5 cages present. We welcomed one "newbie" who wasn't a newbie. Bruce had ridden with the PGR and ALR in Palm Beach, but this was his first mission since moving to Ga, and we were glad to have him.

We held a short briefing in front of the reception area, prior to the families arrival, and I asked Swatt and Sam the Trike man if they would remain at the reception area, and escort the family and the hearse to the pavilion where William's final service was to be held, and they both graciously agreed. The rest of us headed down over the hill, toward Pavilion # 1, still struck by the beauty, the awesome views, the silent white headstone, shining in the hot Ga sun. We parked on the upper drive, above the pavilion, got our flags, walked down the hill thru the trees, to stand in the wonderful shade and await the family's arrival.

Shortly after 12 noon, Swatt gave us the "heads up", and a flag line was quickly formed, and was standing in almost perfect order when Swatt and Sam came into view, the flags on their bikes shining brilliant in the sun. After a brief delay, William was carried by 6 family members into the pavilion, as Winger called the Patriot Guard to attention and to present arms. A short memorial service was held, officiated by the funeral director, personally.

At the conclusion of the service, we held our flag line in place until all the family present had said their final good-byes to William, and after they had cleared the pavilion, I dismissed the Patriot Guard. After the service was concluded, several members of the family went around and shook the hands of all present, and repeatedly said, "Thank you". In those moments when you wonder, is it really worth it, this thing that we do, you look into the tear-filled eyes of a family member of this veteran that we never knew in life, and they shake your hand, and say "Thank you for coming", gotta be the best payday in the world.

Respectfully submitted

David Shreckengost (wild1)

Temporary Ride Captain

Ga. Patriot Guard Riders

Some missions are what we call, 'high-profile', and usually there is a Ride Captain who will jump all over a 'high-profile' mission, but this one fell in my lap, and I was grateful for the experience.

Ride Report, Capt. Ron Kadner, USAF, LEO- 073110

On a hot, humid end of July afternoon in Georgia, the fine Americans that make up this unique organization known as the Patriot Guard Riders came together from all over the state to pay their final respects to another American with a distinguished service record. Capt. Ron Kadner had earned a Silver Star with valor, and two Bronze Stars with valor for his service in Vietnam.

As I pulled into the parking lot at Collins Funeral Home in Acworth, the back-parking area was already awash in red, white, and blue, as bikes were filling up the lower parking area, and trying to take advantage of whatever shade could be found.

After the usual hugs and handshakes all around, Soretoe and I met with the funeral director, to make sure we were all on the same page. A quick briefing was held, and then six bikes rolled out to meet the LEO's that were escorting Ron's family. I was a bit nervous about this part, because I was supposed to ride with them, but my bike wasn't ready to go, but when you can send three Ride Captains and a Mentor as part of that group, you don't have anything to worry about. We welcomed 4 newbie's, experienced riders but on their first PGR mission, and held a short briefing for them.

Family and friends were steadily arriving, and about 12:50 pm we established a flag line at the front of the funeral home, with 14 flags blowing gently in a light breeze that made the oppressive heat seem a bit more bearable. The family arrived at approx. 1:25 pm, escorted by Marietta and Hiram Police, with six PGR bikes flying American, PGR, and Air Force flags. They were a beautiful sight. PGR member, "Chance", resplendent in his Marietta Police uniform, called' Order Arms", and "Present Arms", and every PGR member did so in perfect unison.

After the family had made their way inside, the flag line continued to stand tall, with bottles of water, and cold cloths being distributed by those who had arrived on escort duty, by the always gracious 'Twinkletoes'. The flag line stood down at 2 pm, after over an hour in the scorching heat, with no incidents, thanks to the diligence of the Ride Captains present.

We retired to the shade trees in the rear, to await the honor guard that was to fold the flag for Ron's widow, and offer a 21-gun salute. However, when I inquired again of the funeral director, I learned that the Honor guard from Cherokee County Sheriff's Dept was apparently part of the 'Swat' team, and they had been called out, so all of that part of the service had simply been canceled. After thanking all members present, we waited until the service was over with, then fired up the bikes and departed.

Special thanks to Bill Gaskin (RT) who rode up from Savannah, because he knew Ron, and had grown up with Ron's kids, and had a special reason for coming, that will not be mentioned here. It's always good to have 5 Ride Captains on any mission, Lou, JR, Benny, Mark, RT, good job as always, it's pretty easy to run a mission with guys like you around. And the other members of the PGR, you made me proud once again. Your dedication is beyond my capacity to describe. It is an honor to stand with you, to call you 'brother' and 'sister', and friend. Job well done, all of you.

Mission Complete

Respectfully submitted

David Shreckengost (wild1)

Temporary Ride Captain

I've always had an affinity for motorcycles, I rode a friend's dirt bike for the first time probably around age 12. Never could persuade my parents to buy me one, and quite frankly, they probably could not have afforded one, had they been so inclined, which they were not.

Moved away from home, just short of my 20th birthday, but that desire to feel the "knees in the breeze" never went away, and it was without the consent of ex-wife # 1 that I finally became the proud owner of a Suzuki T – 750, complete with Windjammer fairing. Got it from a friend of mine in exchange for some roof work on a house he was fixing up to sell. The ex-wife was not any happier than my parents would have been, but, what the hey, you can't please everybody.

I got some badly needed experience on that bike, until it developed some serious engine problems, and then I stumbled onto a Suzuki GS-650, on sale. Once again ex-wife was not consulted, but she got over it, eventually. That was one sweet running little machine. Rode it down thru the Keys to Key West, three times. Took it up thru New York, New England, into Canada, five times

With Honor and Respect

CHAPTER 3

RIDE CAPTAIN

On Tuesday, August 3, 2010, it became official, I was promoted to Ride Captain by then State Captain Jeff (Jay Dub) Goodiel. I remember being excited and grateful, but the 'pay' is the same as a mentor, and there is more work involved but I was thankful for the recognition of my services and the official promotion.

A few weeks ago, I submitted David Shreckengost's name to National for promotion to full Ride Captain. Unfortunately, the site went down just as I did that so he was never sent his new security role. I have since resubmitted David's info but I am told that the accounts section of the site is still not fully operational. I was holding off announcing David's new status until it was official but decided it's just silly to continue waiting.

So, because David has gone above and beyond his duties as a mentor and has led several missions as RCIC, and has shown himself as a well-respected leader, it is my pleasure to announce David 'Wild1' Shreckengost as Georgia's newest Ride Captain.

Please adjust your leadership email lists to reflect David as a full Ride Captain.

Thank you Wild1.

Jeff 'JayDub' Goodiel

Georgia State Captain

Patriot Guard Riders

It wasn't long after that, the first mission as a 'real' Ride Captain comes along. A brand-new maroon hat, or as we like to call them, 'moron' hats, and it's time to stand for another veteran, who stood for us, long ago, in a faraway place called Vietnam.

Ride Report- Victor J. Renaud (ret- USA) August 19, 2010

It was a mission that began like many other missions, a phone call saying " we have a veteran here, and the family would like for you to come. Can you come?" Saying 'no, we won't come' never crosses your mind. A veteran, who stood in defense of freedom, has gone home. "Yes, we will come" Information is gathered, phone calls are made. Postings are sent out; postings are made on all sites. More phone calls more information, revised postings, details. Toes has me covered for flags, one item off the list.

On Thursday, August, 19, 2010, dedicated men and women from across Georgia, laid aside their plans, jobs, hobbies, appointments, yard work, and converged on Riverdale, GA to pay their respects to a veteran of 25 yrs. None of them had known Victor (Butch) Renaud in life, but that didn't matter. Victor had served his country for a quarter of a century, including one tour of Vietnam, where he was wounded and received the purple heart.

Seven bikes, one trike and two cages made a total of ten Patriot Guard Riders standing tall when the family arrived just before 10 am. As the family exited the limousine, we all came to attention and presented arms on a silent call. After the family had entered the funeral home, we divided up, with most of us taking up positions on either side of the main entrance, while two members stayed at the side entrance.

At almost every mission, there is that moment, that one special moment, sometimes very fleeting, sometimes lasting longer, but indelibly etched in your mind, and we were about to have such a moment. I had barely taken position on the end of the flag line at the front door, when Keith (KP) Cheeks looked up and said, "What are they doing?"

I looked up to see Pete (Tank 60) Swisher and Lou (sore toe) Costello heading across the front yard of the funeral home, toward the flag pole. One glimpse of the tattered flag on the pole and the new flag that 'toes' was carrying and I knew exactly what they had in mind. It took a few minutes to untie the rope on the pole, and the old tattered flag was lowered. Another minute or two, and a brand-new brilliant flag was hoisted to the top of the mast, and then lowered to half-staff.

When I turned back from taking pictures, the entire assembly of Patriot Guard Riders was at 'present arms', saluting the flag that was wafting gracefully in a gentle breeze. It was a series of moments, done without press coverage, no media spotlight to play to, just two patriots, doing what was right, they didn't ask, they just did it. A moment to remember, or never forget.

We broke down the flag line at 12 noon, and assembled at the side entrance, as the Honor Guard from the Georgia National Guard carried our hero out for the last time. KP and Tank had the honor of riding two of Victor's grandsons with them, as we escorted the hearse and the family up to College Park for the internment. With one LEO bike, and our good friends, Side car Larry, and Gunner, the escort went smoothly.

Upon arriving at the cemetery, we once again set up a flag line at the edge of the drive, just above the tent where the family was gathered. Chaplain de Camp spoke eloquently of Victor's service to his country, his time in Vietnam, and the Chaplain even mentioned to the assembled family that some of the PGR members present were also Vietnam veterans. It was a very subdued but very dignified service, very crisply executed by the Honor Guard. The flag was folded and presented. Two additional flags, already folded, were presented to each of his daughters.

Twenty-one-gun salute, taps, and the service was at its close.

We quietly walked away.

Respectfully submitted

David (wild1) Shreckengost

Georgia Patriot Guard Ride Captain

Sometimes missions go exactly the way you plan, sometimes they don't, but we always try to adjust in whatever manner we need to, to accommodate the family or the funeral home. "Semper Gumby", is our unofficial motto, that's just how we roll.

Ride Report, Eddie Lawrence, September 24, 2010

On a beautiful September afternoon, the Patriot Guard Riders converged on Milledgeville, Ga to pay their respects to Vietnam Veteran Eddie Lawrence. They came from close by, and as far away as Athens, Bethlehem, Stockbridge, Newnan, Warner Robbins. They came, not because they were ordered to do so, they didn't show up to be on the evening news, or get their picture in the paper, they came simply because it was the right thing to do. Eddie Lawrence had served his country during a difficult era, and he didn't get a welcome home, so they came to show his family that Eddie's service did matter, and that there were Americans who just wanted to say "Thank You".

Twelve bikes and two trikes and the all-important flag wagon made their way to Milledgeville. After a short briefing, and recognizing one 'newbie', flag line positions were taken at both entrances to Moores Funeral Home, as a steady flow of family and friends arrived. As always, change was the order of the day, as we had to reposition all bikes once, and then when we finally were able to coordinate with the Funeral Director, we moved bikes again, we were able to cover the four corners of the hearse, as we like to do.

The flag line stood down as the service began, and flags put away, preparing for a quick move once the service was over. The Patriot Guard was in position when Eddie was carried out, and our own Navy veteran, Paul, "Mad Hatter" Long called them to 'attention' and 'present arms'. Then it was jump on the bikes, and a LEO escorted ride to the Ga. Veterans cemetery, just a few miles away.

The flag line quickly re-assembled upon arrival at the cemetery, and Paul once again barked out commands as Eddie was carried into the chapel, escorted by the Honor Guard. As we assembled around the parked bikes, the notes of 'Taps' were played out from the bell tower, and all activity ceased as we turned to face the flag, and whisper a final good-bye to a father, husband, grand-father, veteran. Rest in peace, Eddie, your mission here is complete.

Respectfully submitted,

RC David (wild1) Shreckengost

We have a saying in the Patriot Guard, "However many show up, it's always the right number", and that seems to hold true. You get a mission request, you get the information, try to learn at least a little bit about the person you are honoring, and what their service was. You put the information together, you send it up for posting on the Patriot Guard National Website, you put a post on the Ga State site, and you post it on Facebook, then sit back and hope that someone shows up beside you.

Ride Report, James Leonard Gregory, Monroe Ga Sept 28, 2010

It was a beautiful fall morning in Ga that began with a chill in the air, that was still hanging around when I pulled up in front of Grace Baptist Church. Nothing makes a Ride captain feel better than pulling up and seeing some bikes are already there, and the lovely sight of a flag wagon, and you knew that things were going to go well. Before staging time arrived, two more bikes arrived and we had a good turnout. After a short briefing, we mounted the bikes and drove a short distance to the funeral home, where we were able to pay our final respects to a veteran who had served his country for 29 years.

As James Leonard Gregory was wheeled out to be placed in the hearse, 5 Patriot Guard Riders came to attention and "present arms", and then we mounted up and made the short run back to the church, with the aid of Monroe PD. We arrived back at the church, to find that George and Deddlebug had joined Paul and Pam, and they were in position already. We quickly parked the bikes and joined them, as the family began to arrive. Honors were rendered again as James was carried inside, and then the flag line stood down. "Mad Hatter" and " Keeper of Peace" took the flags and headed off to Athens, to meet us at the cemetery.

After consulting with the Commander of the Monroe Police Dept, we got our bikes lined up, two police cars back of the hearse, but that was their call. As the service ended, we once again rendered honors, and then we were on the road, with outstanding LEO support every inch of the way. City of Monroe, Walton County Sheriff, Oconee County Sheriff, Athens- Clarke County, Georgia State Police, all were outstanding.

At the cemetery, we were once again parking bikes as quickly as possible and taking positions. Nine flags never looked better than they did on that Georgia afternoon, with a slight breeze and beautiful sunshine. A few words from the minister, the Honor Guard steps up, the flag is lifted and held up, a volley rings out, a second, then a third. Then the haunting melody of 'Taps' is heard once again. The flag is folded and presented, and then it's over. We hold the flag line as the family walks away from the grave, then one after another, they walk down the flag line, shaking hands, "Thank you, thank you for being here" again and again you hear those words, and slowly the realization comes, it does matter, it does make a difference. Nine people who never knew this man, were there to say, " We care".

It was a beautiful fall day in Georgia.

Respectfully submitted

David (wild1) Shreckengost

The following mission was unusual in several respects. What had started out as one mission branched off into two, and fortunately we had enough people to do both, respectably.

RIDE REPORT – BRINGING HOME THE FLAG / TONYA BURNS OCT. 16, 2010

It was a mission that began over 900 miles away, when the unclaimed remains of seven veterans were found in the basement of a museum undergoing restoration in Buffalo, NY. The building had previously been a funeral home, and these unclaimed remains had been left in a closet in the basement when the funeral home moved out.

Thru the "Missing In America" project, led by the Patriot Guard, the remains were carried to the National Cemetery in Bath NY on September 24, 2010, where they were laid to rest with full military honors. In order for this to happen, each set of remains had to have consent from the closest kin, and my good friend, Ed Kornowski, PGR member and volunteer part-time genealogist, located a relative for one of these veterans living in Suwanee, Ga. Ed contacted Carlton Sellars, and asked him if he would like to have the flag that had accompanied his uncle, TSgt Osborne Sellars to his final resting place. Carlton said he would be honored to receive that flag, and thus we come to Saturday, October 16, 2010.

Sometimes, it is possible to look back at events that transpire, and realize that God has been working, even in ways we don't understand. The mission of "Bringing the flag home" was originally scheduled to take place on Oct. 9, 2010. However, we were also having a KIA mission in Savannah on that day, and there appeared to be a distinct possibility that protesters were going to be there, so the decision was made to 'stand down', and support the mission in Savannah, which we did, and a hero was laid to rest in Savannah, undisturbed by disgusting hate-mongers.

On Sunday, Oct. 10, we learned the tragic news. ALR/PGR member Al 'WarDog' Burns and his wife, Tonya had been involved in a motorcycle accident in Tennessee. Tonya had been killed instantly and Al was in critical condition. After rescheduling the mission to present the flag to Carlton Sellars on Oct. 16, we learned that a memorial service for Tonya would be the same day, just a few miles north of where we would be, so at Jay Dub's request, the two missions were merged into one.

After staging at the Cracker Barrel, having a great breakfast and welcoming two new members, we got a call from Mr. Sellars that he was running late for our set appointment. At the suggestion of my wonderful girlfriend Elizabeth, we divided our forces, and under the direction of Rick (Claus) Hyman and Larry (Laru) Klein, accompanied by the Mad Hatter with the flag wagon, one group went directly to the funeral home in Buford, to stand for Tonya. I took the other group, and escorted by Gwinnett Sheriff's car, City of Suwanee Police, and Gwinnett County Police, we made our way to Mr. Sellars home.

At approx. 12:30 pm 12 motorcycles rolled into a quiet suburban neighborhood is Suwanee Ga, and pulled to a halt in front of 1XXX Chattahoochee Run Dr. Riders dismounted and came to attention. A very special flag was removed from the saddlebag of the rear bike, driven by Ed (poppy tew) Napoli, PGR mentor. Ed executed a perfect 90 deg turn, and passed the flag to the next PGR member in line, stepped back and saluted. This process was repeated all the way up the line, until Keith (KP) Cheeks handed it to me, then stepped back and saluted. I executed an about-face to the best of my ability and handed the flag to Carlton Sellars, told him it was on behalf of a grateful nation for the service of his uncle, TSgt Osborne Sellars.

Carlton was late arriving for our scheduled transfer, and to be honest, he seemed a bit amused by us being there, but the sight of that flag being handed so carefully down the line, with obvious respect and dignity, by the time I turned to face him, he had tears in his eyes. He was quite emotional as he thanked us profusely for bringing the flag, and for all that we do, and he expressed his thanks to the New York Patriot Guard as well. It was a very simple ceremony, but a very moving one. A special "thank you" goes out to our PGR brothers and sisters in New York for allowing us to finish what they started.

After handshakes and hugs all the way around, the PGR was back on their bikes, rolling north to join our PGR and ALR brothers to pay our respects to Tonya Burns. A beautiful flag line was already in place when we rolled up, just as the service was about to get underway. The flag line stood down, and we remained at ease, until the ALR ride captain summoned everyone to line up along the drive in front of the funeral home, and all present saluted the family as they made the way out. ALR and some of the PGR riders escorted Tonya's family when they departed, the majority of the PGR riders were unable to participate due to other commitments.

Like most missions we do, everything did not happen exactly as we would have wanted to, yet as always, we adapted, and did the very best we could, given the circumstances. A special tip of the hat to Deputy Glen Simmons, Gwinnett County Sheriff's Dept, and Officer Will Johnson, City of Suwanee, great job guys.

A good job all around by the PGR members, we represented ourselves and New York with dignity and class, and honored a fallen sister as well. All in a day's work

Respectfully submitted,

David (wild1) Shreckengost

Ga Patriot Guard Ride Captain.

With Honor and Respect

CHAPTER 4

HERE, THERE, AND EVERYWHERE

When mission requests come into the Patriot Guard today, the mission is sent to one of four Assistant State Captains. Georgia is divided up into four regions, North East, North West, South East and South West, with I – 20 being the dividing line between North and South, and the 400 Corridor and I – 75 being the dividing line between East and West. Back in the "old" days, however, a mission request went out to everyone in leadership, regardless of location, and if you were the first person to jump on, it was yours. Thus, you could find yourself, "here, there, and everywhere".

Ride Report- Roy. F. Blitch – Pembroke, Ga. June 13, 2011

On a morning that dawned clear, sunny and humid, Patriot Guard riders fromacross the Low Country fired up their bikes and headed toward Pembroke, Ga to stand and honor a veteran who had served his country for more than 20 years.

The call to come was from one of our own, Rodney Blitch of Warner Robins, a fellow PGR member, was having to bury his father and it was at his request that riders slipped into the cool morning air, and made their way to Pembroke.

The morning mist had not yet dispelled as they rode the flatlands of coastal Ga, and as they entered the town of Pembroke, they could not help but notice a large field in the center of town, with small white crosses, each cross bearing the name of a serviceman or woman, the conflict in which they had fallen, and an American flag planted next to each cross. It was only fitting, that on this day, as they came to honor another fallen hero, it seemed almost as if the heroes of conflicts past were still there, watching over, and reminding all that freedom was not free.

Sixteen bikes assembled in the parking lot of the Flanders-Morrison Funeral home, one, or two at a time. I had just called the riders together for a short briefing when Rodney and his wife rode up. It was a very emotional moment for Rodney, as he thanked everyone for coming, and we got the opportunity to comfort our brother, as best we could.

A flag line went up at 0900, and 18 flag holders were a beautiful sight in the bright morning sunshine. Flags were brought courtesy of Susie Tompkins from Baxley, along with a cooler full of cold water, and both were vitally important on a day that got hotter and hotter. The Guard was called to 'attention' and 'present arms' as the family arrived. After the service began at 1000, we assembled under the shade trees at the rear of the funeral home, and while waiting, I was able to finalize our LEO escortsn with Chatham and Effingham counties. The Guard assembled again at the sides of the hearse as Roy was brought out, and was called to 'attention' and 'present arms' by Mickey Snelling, Road Captain for the Sons of Liberty.

Bikes were lined up, mounted, and at the signal from "Jersey" of the Bomber Girls, all sixteen bikes fired in unison, and it was a beautiful sound in the morning air. We escorted Roy to the Hillcrest Abbey West Cemetery in Savannah with

LEO escort from Bryan, Effingham, and Chatham County Sheriff's Depts. and they did a superb job. Upon arriving at the cemetery, we re-formed the flag line around the tent, and once again 'present arms' was called, as the Honor Guard carried the casket to its final resting place. Some words from the minister, a short prayer, three volleys into the air, and the mournful sound of taps.

The Honor Guard stacks their weapons, and march back to the side of the coffin, where all 8 of them helped to fold the flag. The flag is presented to Roy's widow, I presented her the condolence book, which was supplied by Pam (keeper of peace) and put together by myself. The flag line is dismissed, we walk back to our bikes, and ride off, by one's or two's, each going their own way, but knowing in their heart that there was no other place that they would have been, then right there where they were, comforting a brother and his family, and for a few moments, showing them that they were not alone. It was an honor to be there, to direct the mission in some small way, and to be a small part of saying "Farewell" to Sgt. Roy F. Blitch.

Respectfully submitted,

David (wild1) Shreckengost

Ride Captain- Patriot Guard Riders

Whenever the phone rings, you never know what it's going to bring, but we go where we need to, because we're the Patriot Guard Riders, and that's how we roll.

RIDE REPORT – RALPH PURDEN GARDEN CITY, GA JULY 20, 2011

When a request is made for us to honor a veteran who has passed way, and therequest comes in from the Commander of an American Legion Post, you know you can't say no, even if that post is 230 miles from where you live. Even before I talked to Bill Helms on the phone, I knew we were going, it was just a matter of getting the details lined up. Sgt. Ralph Pruden had served his country in some extraordinary ways. Bill told me about Ralph being with a unit that was in Spain, and they all had to wear civilian clothes. Ralph had also been in Somalia, and Iraq. So now it was our turn to stand for him, and the Patriot Guard stood proud and tall.

It's always nice to have somebody to ride with, and I was grateful to Asst.State Captain Larry (Laru) Klein, for riding down to Garden City with me. We arrived at the funeral home shortly after 11 am, and had two other riders pull in while we were discussing details with the staff. Mickey Snelling and his sidekick,

Mike went to lunch with us, and when we returned to the funeral home, there were 6 more bikes and one cage there. Several more bikes came in before we got word that it was time to go.

At the request of the family, 6 Patriot Guard Members placed Ralph's casket in the back of the hearse around 1:20 pm, and we lined up bikes for an escort to St. John the Baptist Cathedral in Savannah. We had requested LEO support from

Garden City, and Savannah/Metro police, but had to go without it on the trip into Savannah. I asked Mickey to take the lead, as he is very familiar with the area, and Laru took the back door, and we arrived at St John's without incident.

I had already received a 'heads up' from Susie Tompkins, our 'flag wagoner', that there was no parking to be had, so having noted that there was a very wide sidewalk in front of the Cathedral, I had advised Mickey that we would park the bikes on the sidewalk, and we did.

A flag line was quickly formed, and standing tall when 6 PGR brothers carried Ralph up two sets of steps and into the Cathedral. We normally do not stand a flag line during a funeral service, but I knew this would be our only opportunity to honor Ralph, so I felt it was appropriate, so a beautiful line of red, white, and blue stood proudly in the hot afternoon sun in front of that beautiful Cathedral. We got quite a few glances and lots of pictures taken by passing tourist.

Approx. 45 mins later, the doors open, the service is over, the flag line now switches from the front of the Cathedral, to lining both sides of the entrance, so that as the casket is carried back down the steps, they pass between the flags for the last time. Laru calls everyone to 'attention,' and 'present arms', as we render final honors to another hero. A poem is read, as the family gathers at the back of the hearse, family members release white balloons, and watch them drift skyward. Helmets on, bikes fire up, and move into position. This time we have LEO support from Savannah/Metro, and they did a great job. Down the tree lined streets, across the viaduct, over to Garden City in beautiful fashion, flags brilliant in the afternoon sun. Back to the funeral home, park the bikes, and line up again.

"Attention," "Present Arms", as we place the casket back on its carrier, and it is rolled back into the funeral home.

"Order, Arms" and it's done. Bikes start up and leave, by ones or two's, knowing that for one afternoon, they made a difference, for one family, as they honored an American hero.

Respectfully submitted

David (wild1) Shreckengost

Ride Captain

Patriot Guard Riders

The funerals of Law Enforcement Officers (LEO's) are always difficult ones, we hate to lose any of those who 'protect and serve', but when we do, if asked, the Patriot Guard Riders will be there, even on very short notice.

RIDE REPOT – DEPUTY DERRICK WHITTLE, BLAIRSVILLE, GA 09-20-2011

Even as I sit down almost a week later, to try to compose something relevant to what happened on a day that will truly remain with me as long as I live, I am still in awe of the people who comprise this wonderful organization that we call the Patriot Guard Riders. Union County Deputy Sheriff Derrick Whittle had given his life, responding to a call for help, and we received notice of the families desire for the Patriot Guard to come and honor him, less than 24 hrs. prior to the service, and by the time details were gathered, and finally posted on the national site, we had fewer than 18 hrs. to pull a mission together.

I made numerous phone calls requesting any assistance that could be offered, and the man who stepped forward was Ride Captain Mark (son-in-law) Taylor. Mark immediately offered to bring flags, and he was waiting in the parking lot at First Baptist Church, Blairsville, when I rolled in with Larry (Laru) Klein and Jack (Spook2) Lannen. There were three other bikes already there, and as Mark and I worked out details, more continued to roll in.

Laru, Spook2, JD and myself left the church and went up to Mountain View Funeral Home, and after talking with the funeral director, at the request of the family, the Patriot Guard bikes were placed directly in front of the hearse, which was a tremendous honor and truly speaks volumes about how the Patriot Guard is regarded in that community, and by this family.

When the casket of Deputy Whittle was wheeled out of the funeral home, more than one hundred law enforcement officers from across Georgia came to attention, along with 4 Patriot Guard Riders. The 16 Atlanta Police motorcycle bikes lead the procession down the hill, right turn, 1/4 mile, left turn then left into the church parking lot, not a long procession but a beautiful one. Mark had flags and flag line in place and despite the earlier threat of rain, sunshine was now pouring down.

Needless to say, it took a long time to get everyone into the church sanctuary, and I was told later by one of the custodians that in a sanctuary that had seating for 800 people, they had almost 1100 inside. The flag line stood down as the service began, and Mark gathered up all but the escorting bikes, and headed out to the cemetery, to once again have everything set up.

The procession leaving the church was even more impressive, as the APD motor unit had been joined by Cobb County, Cherokee County, Cartersville, and Hall County. Total, there must have been 40 police motorcycles, and they were in perfect formation as the procession wound its way thru Blairsville and into the country side. As we reached the final turn, that would take us to the cemetery, all the police bikes were lined up, on both sides of the road, in perfect formation, each officer at attention and saluting their fallen comrade. It was truly a beautiful and heart-wrenching sight at the same time, and definitely one I'll not forget.

It's a very small cemetery, surrounded by pasture. Mark has put up static flags, and a flag line, and it looks absolutely beautiful. We peal the bikes off, as the hearse pulls into the cemetery, and we have to park several hundred yards down on the side of the road. There are only four flags left in the back of Mark's truck, all the others are deployed, so we grab those four and take our place in line. It takes a while to get that many vehicles into that small an area, but at last the calls ring out, and Deputy Whittle is carried to his final resting place. A graveside service a bit longer than most, a fly over by a medi-vac chopper, the 21 gun salute by the honor guard from Hall County Sheriff's Dept, the flag is presented, then every Union County officer filed by the family, to shake hands, express their condolences, so we held the flag line until they were through, felt that it was only appropriate.

The last officer has gone thru, a wave of the hand, and the flag line quietly melts away, but not before a number of officers have gone down the line, "Thank you so much", "Thank you for being here", words are spoken with conviction, from the heart, and you realize, once again, why we do what we do. It is not about us, it's all about them, and they were very thankful that we were there.

Flags are rolled up and stowed, good-byes are said, fire up the bikes, lets head for home. For Dan Garland and his wife, for Mongo, and for Heidi, 4 newbies on their first PGR mission, "Thank you", you will never know how much impact your presence had on this day. To everyone who rode, despite the forecast of rain, you are awesome, people, and we could not do this without you. "Thank you, each and every one" and a special thanks to Mark Taylor, who never hesitated, this mission would not have come off without your help. I owe you big time, brother. Truly a memorable mission, job well done, Patriot Guard Riders.

Respectfully submitted

David (Wild1) Shreckengost

Almost no PGR mission comes off without some assistance, and this one was no different. A very simple, straight-forward mission, but with a lot of moving parts, and a Ride Captain has to depend on others to help pull it off.

RIDE REPORT LEON SHUMATE, FOREST PARK, GA 10-14-2011

In what could best be described as "Chamber of Commerce" weather on a beautiful Friday, a dedicated group of Patriot Guard Riders rode into Forest Park to render honor to the life of Leon Shumate. Leon had fought in Germany, and had been captured by the Germans near the end of WW II. We had been alerted to Leon's passing by PGR member Rodney White, who was a close friend of the Shumate family, and came and stood for his friend at visitation and the funeral service.

Visitation on Thursday evening was a quiet, reflective time, as 6 patriots stood and honored a fallen hero. Friday's flag line before the 11 am service was again a respectful, tribute, honoring to Leon and his family. The Patriot Guard was in position when the service concluded, and rendered honors again, as the casket was rolled out to the hearse, with Asst State Captain Larry, "Laru" Klein giving the commands.

With motorcycle escorts, including our own, "Sidecar" Larry, an orderly procession departed for the cemetery in Marietta. Without incident, we arrived at the cemetery, where the military honor guard awaited. A quick grab and go, putting flags together, the flag line went up like we had done this before. The honor guard carries the casket, and again, "Laru" barks out the commands. A few words from the minister, then the honor guard steps forward, they raise the flag and hold it, behind us, three consecutive volleys into the air. The sound of taps comes from behind the flag line, then the flag is folded, presented, and the honor guard marches away.

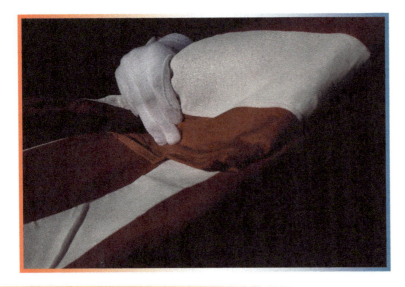

A few more minutes, and the flag lines fades away as well. As we loaded up to go, family members come up and say "Thank you" again and again. There are hugs, a few tears, then we ride away.

A tip of the Ride Captains hat to Larry, Connie, and Bonnie, for providing flags for visitation and funeral service, J Mack McGuigan and Larry Klein, always helping out where ever needed. Everyone who came out, stood tall, rest in the quiet assurance that for this one day, for this one family, you made a difference for them, and they will not forget you. Job well done, Patriot Guard Riders.

Sometimes the simplest missions have the most impact. This one was pretty simple, nothing outstanding about it, but the family was so impressed with those who showed up, and they were so very grateful, you left there with a good feeling in your heart.

Ride Report – Charles Rathel, Jonesboro, Ga 11-09-2011

It was a good day in Jonesboro, Ga. as the Patriot Guard gathered to pay their final respects to a Vietnam Veteran. Larry, Connie and Bonnie were already at Tara Garden Chapel when I pulled in, and there were three bikes there also, including RC Joe, "Mac" McQ. Bikes continued to arrive until we had 11 bikes and 14 flag holders.

A flag line was quickly established, as we were notified that the family was enroute, so the pre-mission briefing was passed over. 14 flags in line, as well as the static flags that Larry and Connie had put out front. It was a beautiful sight. It was a short notice mission, and to have this kind of turnout was wonderful.

We held the flag line for one hour prior to the service, as the body had already been cremated. Charles's daughter-in-law, Diane, came out shortly after the flag line was established, and requested that all the Patriot Guard members present sign the guest book for Charles, she asked us to sign on the page for pall bearers, and we were honored to do so. Several family members approached various Patriot Guard members and expressed their thanks for our presence, and those sentiments were shared with all present.

When the service began at 2 pm, we broke down the flag line and rolled them up. We then had a post mission briefing, recognizing one new member, Bill, who was actually on his second mission. We recognized the veterans, and Vietnam veterans who were present, said the Pledge of Allegiance, a brief prayer and then a quiet roll down the driveway, and fire up the engines away from the funeral home.

Mission Completed, well done, Patriot Guard Riders.

My last mission as Ride Captain for the year 2011 is truly one of the most memorable that I will ever have the chance to participate in. Say the name 'Larry Munson' in the State of Georgia, and you are truly talking about a living legend. Everyone in Georgia, regardless of race, creed or color knows that name, so when the Patriot Guard Riders were asked to come to Athens, Ga, and stand for this legendary character, we jumped at the chance.

RIDE REPORT - LARRY MUNSON, ATHENS, GA 12-14-2011

On a beautiful late fall afternoon in Athens, Ga. the Patriot Guard gathered to honor the service of Sgt. Larry Munson, a medic in an Army hospital during WW II. While most of us, especially those who are University of Georgia Bulldog fans, knew Larry Munson as the "legendary voice of the Bulldogs" for 43 yrs., Lawrence Harry "Larry" Munson, as a young man, stepped forward, raised his right hand, and stepped into the service of his country.

For that and his service as a medic, Larry Munson forever more became an American hero.

Dr. Kelly (Teach) Whittaker did a great deal of leg work on this mission, and kudos to her are definitely in order. She met with the Assistant Athletic Director on several occasion and recon'ed Sanford Stadium. She also met with Director of Parking, and the Campus Police, and secured us an awesome reserved parking area, which is no easy feat around Sanford Stadium.

Patriot Guard Riders from across the state rolled into Athens, in groups, or singly, and by the time came for our 11:30 briefing, 30 riders were present. We were joined by a couple of newbies, two of whom were students at UGA, and Ride Captain Jim Gordon's entire family was present to stand the flag line with him for the first time.

Keith Cheek and Teach had a brief mentor meeting, as the remainder of the PGR walked across the street, and down the ramp, under Sanford Stadium. We got to share the visitors' locker room with the Honor Guard from Ft. Gordon, but most were interested in getting their photo taken inside this illustrious facility. Flags were provided by our own Ga Waterboy, Bill Dowden and the Honor Guard especially enjoyed Bill's back door 'buffet'.

The flag line was led onto the field by RC Jim Gordon at approx. 12;20 pm, as the video screen played a 40-minute tribute to Larry, while fans filed into the South side of the stadium. This was my first visit to Sanford Stadium and to be able to walk on that field, and stand with my back to the famous 'hedges' was way beyond cool.

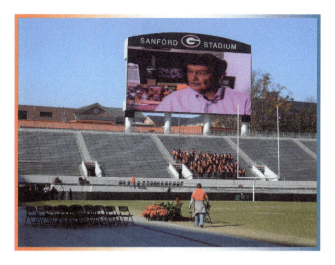

At approx. 1 pm, the Munson family, led by sons Johnathan and Michael, emerged from under the stands and walked to the waiting chairs at the 50 yd line. I called the Patriot Guard to attention, and to present arms, as the family walked past. Scott Howard, Mark Richt, Vince Dooley, they were all there, and all remember Larry. His sons Johnathan and Michael spoke eloquently about their dad, growing up in the Munson household, and telling stories we would never have heard anywhere else.

The Honor Guard rendered the 21-gun salute, the University of Georgia Redcoat Band had a trumpeter play taps and the service was over. The family got up, and walked off the field. Despite the rather cool temperatures, those present, with only one exception, had held their positions, almost unmoving, for almost two hours. It was one of the most beautiful, quiet, respectful flag lines I have ever had the privilege of being a part of. The Patriot Guard truly put its collective "best foot" forward, and I was proud of each and every one of them.

Kudo's also the Hi-Tech Redneck, David Andrews, a '60 UGA grad, who made this his first mission back since shoulder surgery, a tip of the hat to George and Deedle, who had also done some recon work, but they had to leave early. All around great mission, awesome turnout by the most wonderful people on this planet, the men and women of the Ga Patriot Guard Riders.

Respectfully submitted

David (Wild1) Shreckengost

Ride Captain, Ga. Patriot Guard Riders

CHAPTER FIVE

ANOTHER YEAR

Some missions are pretty easy, all you have to do is show up. As a Ride Captain you love those kinds of missions, and this one fell right into that category.

Ride Report - Deployment Ceremony, 3rd MCDS. Det 36 Jan. 19. 2012

When the request came in from Colonel Baldwin, asking for the Patriot Guard to come and stand for his detachment, as they were about to deploy, all we could say was, "where and when?" While we wish that none of these fine men and women had to leave their families and their friends behind, we understand that they do it to protect the freedom we hold dear, and it was on honor for us to be a part of their deployment ceremony.

Twelve Patriot Guard Riders roared up in front of Building 900 at Ft. Gillem in the bright January sunshine. Flags are unfurled and carried inside, where we were greeted like long lost relatives. We got to mingle with the troops for a few minutes before Sergeant Major Moody assembled the detachment, and the ceremony was underway.

A wonderful rendition of the national anthem, (acapella), an opening prayer from the Chaplain. Colonel Baldwin stepped to the podium, and delivered a brief but heartfelt address to the assembled family members and the members of his detachment. He also presented a certificate of appreciation to Ga. State Patriot Guard Captain Jeff "JayDub" Goodiel, thanking the Patriot Guard for being there, and for what we do on a regular basis. A benediction by the Chaplain, and the ceremony was over. But it wasn't over.

We stacked our flags against the wall, and got the opportunity to say "Thank you" personally to many of the soldiers' present, many of whom wanted to thank us for what we do. It was one of the most enjoyable missions that we have had, and the cake and the punch certainly didn't hurt either. After a sufficient time passed, we gathered our flags, said good-bye to some outstanding Americans, and headed outside. There were smiles all around as we loaded up, and roared back out the gate. We will remember our afternoon at Ft. Gillem for a long time, and the members of Det 36, 3rd MCDS will be in our prayers until they are safely home again.

This was truly " a feel good " mission, and I couldn't have been prouder of the Patriot Guard Riders who came out today.

Thank you, everyone, job well done, mission completed.

Sincerely

David (Wild1) Shreckengost

Sometimes the hardest missions are the ones where you get to know the family of the veteran, or in this case, the Active Duty Hero. I refer to all of them as Heroes, because without them, and the sacrifices they make, sometimes including their life, we would not have the freedom to live our lives in peace. I got two Active Duty Heroes, back to back, and got to see up close and personal the pain that these families went through as they said their final 'good-byes' to their sons, their own personal Heroes, and my Heroes as well.

RIDE REPORT - A1C Stephen Robert Bost, Conyers, Ga March 23, 2012

There sometimes does not seem to be sufficient words to adequately describe all the emotions, feelings, and reactions that go into an honor mission. In the last two days, the Patriot Guard has become very well acquainted with the family of A1C Stephen Bost, and we've shared in their pain and shed some tears alongside them as they laid their 22-yr. old son to rest. It was, as his father Joe told me, "the phone call you never want to get". The pain in his voice was very evident even over the telephone as we talked on Wednesday evening about the Patriot Guard, and what the family would like us to do. But, in the long run, the only thing that mattered to this family was that we were there, and they knew that we cared for them, and we wanted to honor their sons service to our country.

Ten faithful Patriots rolled into Horace Ward Rockdale Chapel parking lot on a beautiful Thursday evening. The forecast was for rain, but they stood for two hours, without a drop falling from the sky. Even as we gathered for a short briefing, we were joined by Stephen's scout master, who talked about Stephen's days in scouts, and what a good kid he was.

Flags were provided by Connie and Larry Harbuck, and Larry set up a static line of flags along Hwy 138 that alerted everyone passing by, that something special was going on. The flag line was set up about 10 minutes early, as a steady procession of visitors had already begun. With a back drop of cherry blossoms and a fading sunset, the line remained virtually unwavering thru out. The usual cadre of Air Force personnel, coming and going, some stopping to shake hands, say thank you, and us in return thanking them, for the freedom we enjoy every day.

Both of Stephens Grand-Fathers stepped outside to thank us for being there. Stephens Squadron Commander, Colonel Rodriguez made a point of shaking every one's hand. At one point, I almost thought I was running for office, I had shaken so many hands. Those who wished to, slipped inside, one at a time, and signed the remembrance book, and as the sun disappeared below the western horizon, we stood our flags next to the door, and went inside as a group to pay our respects.

We were able to gather with Stephen's parents, Joe and Kathleen, and his older brother Joe, and shared with them our sympathies. Don Thuman summed it up better than anyone, as Kathleen was asking us where we were from, and why we were doing this for them, and Don's response was spot on, he said, "When your son stepped forward and raised his hand, he became one of us, he's one of our brothers". That seemed to resonate with this grieving family, and they understood a little better what this meant to all of us. Hugs, handshakes, and a few tears, and we departed, wishing nothing more than that we could wave a magic wand and take away all of the pain that this family was going through.

Friday's weather forecast was for scattered rain, with thunderstorms by mid-afternoon. Not what I wanted to hear, knowing we had a 2 pm service. But weather doesn't keep the Patriot Guard from doing what they do best, and they turned out despite the forecast, to support a grieving family, and to honor a young man who they had never met. 22 Patriots, including 'Poppa Joe' Black, along with TSgt David Hendley and several of Stephens squad mates from Moody AFB rode up to salute their fallen comrade. Bill Dowden had taken over flag duties, and put out a beautiful static flag line in front of the church and along the driveway.

When the hearse arrived carrying Stephen, TSgt Hendley, Sgt Long and another member of Stephens squad lifted one side of the casket, and three Air Force non-coms in uniform were on the other side. The Patriot Guard rendered honors as the flag draped coffin was slowly rolled inside. A short briefing, and the flag line is set up, just in time to have to adjust again, as the rain began to come down, lightly at first, but increasingly heavier. Lines were changed, and everyone managed to squeeze under the side portico.

Again, a steady stream of friends and family walked in between the flags, some shaking hands, all of them saying 'thank you' as they passed thru. Thankfully, by the time the flag line broke down, shortly after 2 pm, the rain had disappeared, and skies appeared to be clearing somewhat. Stand down time is spent, shuffling bikes into position, pushing one here, another one over there, keeping voices low, talking of old missions, people and places. A heads up from one of the funeral directors, and the Patriot Guard is in line and manning the doors, as the same pallbearers place their friend back in the hearse for the last time. The doors close, motors fire up, a wave of a hand, and we're rolling. Rockdale County motor unit out front, our own 'Smokey Squirrel' in the back.

The ride to Fairview is a thing of beauty. Blue lights, Red white and blue flags, mixed with the yellow and blue of the Patriot Guard, the royal blue of the United States Air Force, cherry blossoms falling almost like snow in places. Down the hill, over Honey Creek, right on East Fairview, thru the 4-way stop at Union

Church, as the Rockdale Motor unit turns circles in the intersection. Across Hwy 155, as a Henry County Deputy stands at attention. Downhill again,

past the park, two elementary schools, school buses pulled aside, then the final left turn and down the hill, past the waiting honor guard, their eyes straight ahead, white gloves, perfect uniforms. Park the bikes, grab a flag. Poppa Joe's already in the lead, setting the line on three sides of the two green canvas shelters. An order, barely audible from where we are, and the Honor Guard moves forward. Slowly, with precision, they lift Stephens casket, turn and begin the slow walk to the awaiting grave site. Halt, another turn, and it is in place.

The family takes their places under the green awnings, and almost on cue, a gentle rain begins to fall. The chaplain says a few words, a prayer, another command. Rifles are racked, and shots ring out. and again, and again. With the first notes of taps, the rain seems to stop, almost as if Heaven is saying that the time for tears is over. The flag is folded, presented to Stephens widow, and another is given to his mother. The Honor Guard leaves the field, a few more words from the minister, and the service is over. Flags are rolled up, stowed away. Good-byes are said, some more "Thank you's", motors fire up, and we ride away, singly, twos or threes, each of us wishing we could wave a magic wand and make it all go away.

Respectfully submitted,
David (Wild1) Shreckengost
Ride Captain, Patriot Guard Riders

My next mission wasn't any easier. Brandon Goodine was a McDonough boy, and as a former resident of McDonough, Ga: this one hit close to home. It's also one of the few missions that I've really second-guessed myself, and wish that we had done some things different, but an obstinate Funeral director got in the way, and I felt, as the Ride Captain, I should have done more to run the mission the way it was planned, but we also say, "It's not about us". If we ride in the rear of the procession, so be it. Thankfully, the CAO (Casualty Assistance Officer) chewed her ass out good, and we had no further problems.

RIDE REPORT – BRANDON GOODINE, JUNE 18, 2012

Brandon Goodine. He was the kid next door. We all knew him, even though we had never met him. He was the one that was always on the go. Even in school, his teachers had to keep after him to pay attention. Brandon was "full bore" as his momma would say. Everything he did was "balls to the wall" and he tried to be the best at everything he did. He won awards with his JROTC rifle team.

When he joined the United States Army, he again tried to excel in everything that he did. Brandon had never been on an airplane before he joined the army, and was scared to death of flying. But Brandon did not let that stop him. He overcame his fears when he joined the 82nd Airborne, and the very first plane that Brandon flew on, was also the first plane he jumped out of. Brandon was just that kind of guy. He was the scout for his platoon in Afghanistan, which meant he was the man out front, and Brandon was out front of his squad on 7 June, 2012, when a coward that would not face him 'man to man' detonated an IED.

Brandon Goodine. We might think of him as a 'kid', but he was a full-grown warrior, had already been accepted to Ranger school, just a few days after his 20th birthday. And one month to the day after he turned 20 yrs. old, a small charter plane touched down in Peachtree City, Georgia, and Brandon Goodine was home.

It was a beautiful summer morning in Georgia. A bit cool for riding motorcycles, a touch of fog in some low-lying areas, dew glistening on every blade of grass, as patriotic Americans began to gather at Falcon Field. Just a few at first, then a few more. A familiar rumble was heard in the still morning air, and the Southside Riders from Griffin Ga came over the hill, 36 bikes strong, riding in to honor a fallen hero.

Even as they were getting parked, another group roared down the hill, past the monument of the F-16 Falcon. Brandon's dad, Dewayne, rode with the Christian Motorcycle Association Chapter from Newnan, and they had turned out in force to stand for their brother's son. Bikes continued to come, by twos, threes, and more. The parking lot was filled to overflowing and you knew it was going to be a good day. A briefing was conducted, and Dewayne's pastor, TJ, gave a spirit filled invocation asking God's blessings on our mission. A new riders briefing was conducted by Al Reger, as Ride Captains "Hound", "JR" and "Mack" and "Flasher" directed placement of the flag line in anticipation of the arrival of Brandon's family.

The family arrived, escorted by Henry and Fayette County Sheriff's deputies, and officers from Henry County police. They passed thru an almost solid wall of patriots and flags, over 130 strong, lining both sides of the roadway, and pulled directly onto the tarmac. Before the last family vehicle had even stopped rolling, the small Kalitta charter jet had touched down, and begun its roll up. As the plane taxied to a stop, two lines of flags moved down the hill, past the Peachtree City Fire Dept truck with the flag hanging high on the extended boom, behind the LEO's, and family vehicles, and not stopping until the entire assembly had been completely surrounded with the red, white, and blue.

The dignified transfer ceremony was executed flawlessly by the Kalitta crew, and the 82nd's Honor Guard, as a silence that was almost deafening settled over the tarmac. The hearse door is closed, the family is making their way back to their vehicles, the flag line is dismissed, and begins the walk back uphill. Flags are returned to their proper places, courtesy of Connie and Larry Harbuck, and Bill Dowden. Bikes are fired up, as a short "woop" of a police siren tells us the procession is under way.

A last-minute change leaves us standing and watching as all the family vehicles proceed out ahead of us, by the time the first motorcycle pulls out, the hearse is out of view, but it doesn't matter. We're here to honor a fallen hero, and in honor we ride. Two perfect lines of motorcycles, as far as you can see. Passing numerous groups of people who have come out to show Brandon's family that their sacrifice is felt by many. Past Starrs Mill, thru Fayetteville, a route that feels very familiar to those who rode these same roads almost three years to the day, as Sgt. John Beale came home for the last time. Down the hill, over I-75, under another flag hoisted by the City of McDonough Fire Dept, make the turn at the square. Jammed with people, an outpouring of love and support that Brandon certainly deserved. The final left turn into the funeral home, bikes jockeying for the limited parking spaces. We dismount, only to find that the Honor Guard has already taken Brandon inside, and we're a bit disappointed that we did not have the opportunity to render honors, but it is what it is, and we have done the best we could.

A fine group of patriots made their way back to McDonough on a very warm Sunday afternoon, to stand a flag line for visitation. In anticipation of large crowds, the funeral home had closed off the front entrance, and was directing everyone to the side entrance, which put our flag line directly in the hot sun, so "Hound" and I made the decision to stand the flag line in shifts, and this worked out well for everyone involved. Changes were made at 15-minute increments, and those not standing had shade to sit in, and cold water provided by Connie and Larry, again.

Monday, June 18, 2012 dawned with the promise of a beautiful day, and held true to form. Sixty-three motorcycles found their way to Bethany Baptist Church in McDonough. Larry Harbuck, and his son, Cody, an active duty Marine, had set up a beautiful static line in front of the church, and with all the patriots that had gathered, we were able to extend our flag line from the side entrance, to the front entrance, a beautiful line of red, white and blue, a slight breeze helping to keep the colors flying.

Police activity at the intersection alerts us that the procession is enroute, and then the "woop, woop" of a short siren blast, and the procession comes into view. Atlanta Police and Henry County motorcycle units, in tight formation, a sheriff's car, and then the hearse, with 4 perfectly position PGR motorcycles. "Mack", "Gator", "Jimdawg" and "RedK" with flags flying, were a beautiful sight. The procession stops, the hearse is held in waiting, Major General Donohue leads the family into the church, flags gleaming on either side. A large number of family has gathered, and it takes a few minutes to get everyone inside. The General returns, a nod to the Lieutenant in charge of the Honor Guard, and Brandon is carried thru the red white and blue. We break down the flag line as the service begins, and Larry and Paul get their flags put away and then head for the cemetery, to prepare for arrival there. Everyone else is looking for shade, and some cold water. Almost an hour passes, before we get a 'heads up', and quickly assemble, two and three deep, at the side entrance. The church doors open, Will "Boots" Duke calls the Patriot Guard to 'attention' and 'present arms' as the Honor Guard once again flawlessly executes their duties.

The hearse door closes, everyone mounts their bikes, and on command, all the motorcycles fire as one, a beautiful sound in the warm Georgia air. The LEO motor's pull out, the Patriot Guard falls in behind, with Gail "Flasher" Sorrows directing traffic. A slow, solemn procession rolls down North Bethany Road, makes a left turn onto McGarity, and then a left into the Eastlawn Cemetery. Static flags line the road way, bikes are quickly parked and waiting flags grabbed, as the flag line almost magically reassembles. "Boots" again barks out the commands, and the flag line is straight and true. The chaplain has a few words, commands are once again barked out, a volley, another, then a third. The first notes of taps sound in the warm afternoon air, and an audible sob is heard by all. The flag is perfectly folded, transferred to General Donohue, and presented on one knee to Brandon's widow, Nicole.

The Lieutenant brings a second flag, touches it to the casket, transfers it to the General, then a third, and a fourth. A brief pause then myself and Joe "Mack:" McGuigan step under the green tent. A small teddy bear with a 'mission complete' pin for Brandon's daughter, Hailey. A plaque for father, Dewayne. A condolence book and a plaque for mother, Mandy, another condolence book and a plaque for widow, Nicole, and I stepped back and saluted, thinking to myself that this was one of the hardest things I've ever done.

The chaplain goes down the front row, shaking every one's hand. Nicole places a white rose on the casket, Mandy places Brandon's bible next to it, and the service is over. The flag line quietly fades away, flags are rolled and stowed, bikes fire up and leave, as quietly as is possible, and I feel like I can breathe again.

A special "Thank You" goes out to Pam " Keeper of Peace" for the beautiful condolence books. Thank you also to our outgoing State Captain, JayDub, who immediately said yes when I asked to order two extra plaques. Thanks also to "Mack", who informed me that he is not "jmack", he was a great help, especially with the Monday morning escort. Thanks to Al "Gator" Reger, our Ride Captain in Training, who got lessons in how not to do it, and all the other ride captains who came out and assisted. "Hound", "JR", "Flasher" "Boots" "Airborne", "JJ" "RedK" "Jimdawg", you all helped out in so many different ways. A tip of the hat to Dennis Scott and the Southside Riders, and the Newnan CMA chapter, both groups were a big part of the mission. It was an honor to be able to stand for Brandon, to meet his family and get to know them a little better. It was a learning experience and lessons learned will definitely be applied to future missions. A special thank you to MSG. Brady, the CAO, a fine soldier who assisted greatly in smoothing out some rough spots.

Without the dedicated members whose names don't get mentioned here, none of this would have been possible, and I salute each and every one who participated in any way, your dedication to our military men and women is what inspires all of us to keep doing this. You show up, standing respectfully, and then ride away, and you are what makes this organization the outstanding body that it is, and I am honored and humbled to stand beside you.

Job well done, Patriot Guard Riders.

Respectfully submitted

David (wild1) Shreckengost

Ride Captain, Georgia Patriot Guard Riders

The engines on the bikes had barely had time to cool off, before the Patriot Guard Riders were on the move again. This one was really personal; this was one of our own. Bonnie Brown Clough was the mother of Connie Harbuck, who, along with her husband, Larry, were one of our main flag wagons in the South Atlanta area. Bonnie had passed away early in May, but her family waited for her nephew to get home from the Marines before they decided to carry her ashes down to St. George Island, and honor her last wishes. Ride Captain for this mission was David (Hound) Blanton, who was at that time the Assistant State Captain for the Southeast Georgia Region.

Ride Report

Transfer Escort Bonnie Brown Clough McDonough, GA to Apalachicola, FL

This mission commenced at the conclusion of Bonnie's service back on May 13 when Connie told us that they would be taking Bonnie's Cremains back home to the Apalachicola, Fl area when their Marine, Bonnie's grandson and Connie's son, Cody was able to get home. Wild1 and I both agreed that it was only fitting that we become involved in assisting the family on their endeavor to take Bonnie home and told Connie and Larry that we would be there with them to assist. We had a tentative date towards the end of June set when the family would be ready.

Many of us got to know Bonnie through our missions with the Patriot Guard Riders. If the Harbuck flag support vehicle was present at a mission, you could bet that Bonnie was there present with Connie and Larry supporting the mission. Bonnie was a quiet shy lady with a deep love of this country and its military, especially proud of her Marine grandson Cody. Bonnie fell in love with the PGR mission and took all of us in as part of her extended family that she cared for very deeply and it was very evident with her smile and greeting to all at every mission. I had the pleasure of friending Bonnie on Facebook and it became part of my morning ritual exchanging greetings and good mornings with her every morning as well as other family and close friends. Suddenly with no warning she was no longer there. It was a time of personal sadness when we learned that Bonnie has passed away in her sleep peacefully and God had another angel at his side. After Bonnie had passed, Connie told me Bonnie had a deep desire to ride a scooter with one of us but was too shy to ask. We all have regrets to unfinished business when we lose someone and this is one that struck me that if I only knew I would have been so willing to satisfy that wish.

Shortly after the first week in June, Connie provided me with the details of when all the family and friends of Bonnie would be present and I started working up a mission to do the Transfer Escort of Bonnie from McDonough, GA to St George Island at Apalachicola, FL. We decided on 5 segments with rest and fuel stops to allow Riders in and out on segments for those unable to make the entire trip and for "pet stops" for family pets accompanying the Harbucks. Harry Trawick volunteered his services when I requested information on passing through Tallahassee and Squirrel offered his escort service the whole trip when he learned of the mission. The FL PGR offered their assistance through Ride Captain Joe Parmer on the Florida segment of the Transfer Escort. I had talked with several Ride Captains and I knew they would be participating so I waited until the morning of the mission to inform them they would lead various portions of the segments as well as carry Bonnie on their segments. I knew I could count on them to take on these responsibilities and in typical PGR fashion they accepted and did an outstanding job. I made a call to PGR member and Dooly County SO LEO Rick Culpepper for assistance in getting us through the construction zone in Dooly County on I-75 which he came in from vacation and provided for us.

This mission was unlike any other PGR mission that I have participated in as planning involved two days with bikes, boats and storming a beach at little St George Island that had no docks. We were able to arrange for a group rate at a local motel for those staying overnight to complete the second phase of the mission of spreading Bonnies ashes on Little St George Island. Connie Harbuck lined up 3 boats to ferry us over through family and friends in the area. Our plans were laid out and on Thursday morning, June 21 we gathered up at Quik-Trip in McDonough to start our mission.

Thursday started out with clear blue skies with it going to be hot during the day with a chance of thunder storms once we hit the panhandle area. As I pulled into the Quik-Trip parking lot an hour early our escort members were already present including the Harbuck family. Big Don rode up from Gray with me and we picked up Festus in Forsyth who rode all the way up from Tifton. Poppa Joe was present riding up from Valdosta that morning. After greetings and such we conducted a brief mission briefing and heading out at 10 AM lead by the Squirrel Cage. We had 10 scooters, 2 cages and the hero escort vehicle. We were on our way on a 324-mile trek to take Bonnie home.

At each segment we had riders join in and most of them rode to the start of the Florida segment. Thanks to Sid, we arrived at each segment within 5 minutes of ETA and not late for a single point. We arrived at the Florida segment 15 minutes earlier due to padding for Tallahassee traffic and Harry's lead and assistance getting us through with no delays or problems. We hit the remainder of a thunderstorm with only a drizzle following a heavy rain near Crawfordville south of Tallahassee for the only liquid sunshine we seen on the trip. When we hit Tallahassee, it seemed the temperature jumped up 20 degrees with it being really hot and most of us looking for sunscreen that made the entire trip. The rest of the trip can be summed up in two words.... Hot and Humid.

We arrived at the beach house on St George Island the Harbucks had rented right on ETA. We did a transfer of Bonnie back to family there, our portion of the Transfer Escort being complete. Those not staying overnight departed to return to their homes while those staying over secured their hotel reservations. After securing our hotel rooms for the night, we returned to the beach house after checking out the ferry site to determine the suitability of scooter parking for grilled hamburgers and hotdogs prepared by the Harbuck family. I think even Outlaw got filled up with the amount of food prepared. It was a good gathering of the family and the PGR with new friendships formed. The wind had started picking up late evening due to a tropical disturbance forming out in the Gulf so we knew we were in for a little chop in the bay on the ferry over. The last time I was in Apalachicola deep sea fishing we faced a day of 8 to 12-foot swells and I swore then that I would never get on another boat in Apalachicola when the wind was blowing. We find we do what we need to do although I knew to pick out the biggest boat to ride on.

Friday morning broke with overcast skies and the wind having let up a little bit compared to the night before and we assembled at the ferry site where we meet more family members and prepared to ferry over to Little St George Island. As we proceeded to cross the bay, the sun came out and burned off the clouds and we crossed with a two-foot chop which wasn't too bad with the speed we were running. Once we got to Little St George Island, we took off our boots and socks to wade through mid-thigh water to reach land since the docks were never replaced since the last hurricane down there and the boats had to anchor off shore from the beach.

Once we reached shore, we conducted a brief ceremony with Connie reading some memories to family and friends while the PGR stood with flags for our sister Bonnie. I know now why Bonnie liked that spot. It was beautiful and so peaceful. After the spreading of Bonnie's ashes, we made a cross out of driftwood and left it along with a picture of Bonnie with an American flag to mark the spot. We had brought Bonnie home to the place she loved and our mission was complete. Pictures tell the story well, much better than I can express in words, of the love and care we all have for Bonnie and I invite you to catch these moments with the images we captured for the family.

Mission Accomplished

David "hound" Blanton

Ride Captain SE Region

Patriot Guard Riders of Georgia

The next mission that I was Ride Captain for was also a personal one, as the call had come from a lady in our church, who was Active Duty military herself, and whose son and daughter had both served under the leadership of Sr. Chief Staats in JROTC.

Ride Report - Senior Chief Gregory Staats, Dallas Ga, Sept. 15, 2012

It was a day that dawned, beautiful and clear, with just a touch of chill in the air, as a reminder that fall was not far away. A day that you knew was going to be perfect for throwing a leg over, firing up the V-twins and taking off for parts unknown. Patriot Guard Riders from across N Georgia did just exactly that, but they had a mission and a purpose when they hit the road, for this was a special day, a day for honor, respect, and to say good-bye to a USN Senior Chief Petty Officer who had served his country, had fought the good fight, and had finished his race.

Fourteen bikes and twenty-one flag holders made their way to the Fortified Hills Baptist Church, to stand on the flag line for Senior Chief. We were joined there by PGR Ride Captain Karen Trone, from Jacksonville, Fl. Her niece had been in the JROTC program under Senior Chief, and Karen had met him several times as she had attended various JROTC functions that her niece was involved in, and she felt lead to come and stand in his honor.

The Corps of Cadets from Union Grove High School arrived by school bus, lined up, and marched in formation into the church. They were a very sharp looking group of future leaders, and it was obvious that Senior Chief had taught them well. Military personnel from all branches of the service, both active duty and retired streamed into the church, for Senior Chief's reputation was well known, and it was fitting that he be so honored.

Service began at 1 pm, and the flag line was dismissed. All present assisted "Pappy" in getting up the large number of static flags that he had set out, and then Pappy and "Balljoint", along with "Captain Bob" headed to the cemetery to prepare for the arrival there. The remaining riders gathered in whatever shade could be found and waited. And waited, and waited, and waited. Almost two full hours passed before the service finally concluded, and when we lined up to escort the family to the cemetery, there were only eight bikes left, as others had departed for other commitments.

Our own Dan O'Keeffe was our only escort for the eight-mile ride to the cemetery, and he did a Yeomans' job in getting everyone there, intact. Larry Klein ran the sweeper position and helped keep the cars in order. Flags were already in place, as Pappy and company were on top of things, as always. We pull in and park, grab a flag and quickly line up. The small cemetery quickly fills with cars, the bus carrying the Corps of Cadets has to park up the hill, and the cadets make their way down to the graveside. The naval honor guard carries the cremains to the graveside, and stands at attention. A few words from the pastor, a prayer, and the honor guard unfolds the flag, hold it up, and those familiar but haunting notes of taps ring across the sunlight headstones, as flags flutter in the slight breeze. The flag is folded, presented, the honor guard marches away in perfect step.

The flag line remains for a few more minutes, then quietly fades away. Laru retrieves the condolence book, and I asked Karen Trone to present it to Senior Chiefs' widow, Vicki. Karen did so most graciously, and the moment they shared was truly special. Flags are rolled, stowed away, and one by one, bikes ride out the drive, some turn left, some turn right, and another mission is complete.

Respectfully submitted,
David (Wild1) Shreckengost
Ride Captain, Patriot Guard Riders

A little humorous incident, if you will indulge me. Probably about a month prior to this mission, I had attended a mission at a Catholic church in Marietta, Ga, were "Soretoe" was the Ride Captain. As best I remember, it was an 11 am service, after which the church was serving lunch to all in attendance, prior to going to the cemetery for the burial service. Once we broke down the flag line, I had some time on my hands and made my way to the fellowship hall, where the luncheon was being prepared. I introduced myself to the ladies that were busy getting things together, and I told them that I could tell immediately when I stepped in the door that this was not a Baptist church. They wanted to know how I could tell, and I informed them that there was no fried chicken, therefore, I knew immediately that this was not a Baptist church. They got quite a chuckle out of that.

Fast forward to Sept. 15, Fortified Hills Baptist Church, similar circumstances. Service, followed by lunch in the Fellowship Hall. Flag line breaks down at the start of the service, I once again made my way back to where the food was being prepared. Opened the door to the Fellowship hall and knew immediately that I was at a real Baptist church, because the first thing you could smell was fried chicken. I had to share with the ladies there my experience with the Catholic church in Marietta, and they got a good laugh out of it as well. Even in the somber business of honoring those who have passed on, you sometimes can find a little humor.

Sometimes, there is no humor in what we do. This was one of those times.

Darryl Mills, Fayetteville, Ga Nov. 29, 2012

On October 31st, and Nov 1, 2010, the Patriot Guard stood in honor of Nathan Ryan Mills of Fayetteville, and escorted him to his final resting place in Canton.

Today, it is my sad duty to inform you that Nathan's brother, Darryl, an eight-year veteran of the United States Army will be laid to rest in Canton alongside his brother, on Thursday, Nov. 29, 2012. Darryl was at his brother's funeral two years ago, and I remember shaking his hand, expressing my condolences for the loss of his brother, and thanking him for his service.

Now it is time for the Patriot Guard to once again support the Mills family in this hour of grief. We will meet at the same funeral home where we stood for his brother, and we will again do a hero's escort to Georgia National Cemetery in Canton.

Staging - 0845 hrs. Thursday, Nov. 29, 2012

Mowell Funeral Home

180 N Jeff Davis Dr. Fayetteville, Ga 30214

We will stand a flag line in silent honor until the service begins.

Escort - 1100 hrs. depart Funeral Home in Fayetteville with escort

Service - 1300 hrs. Georgia National Cemetery, Canton Ga.

RCIC - David (wild1) Shreckengost

wild1handy@yahoo.com

If I wrote a Ride Report for this mission, it has been lost in the years since. But sometimes missions are too hard, I know this one was, this family lost two sons in just over two years' time, and maybe, just maybe, this one was a little too hard to put into words.

Weather is often a factor when it comes to planning missions, and when you have one just before Christmas, even in Georgia, it can get downright cold. But the Patriot Guard Riders are a resourceful bunch, and manage to show up regardless.

Ride Report, John Michael Thomas Collins, 21 Dec 12

We have a saying in the Patriot Guard, something to the effect, "no matter how many people show up at a mission, it's always the right number" and that certainly proved to be the case on a very cold, windy Friday in December. I arrived at the South Canton Funeral Home about 20 mins early, expecting to see at least a couple of bikes or cages already there, only to discover that I was the first PGR member present.

As a Ride Captain, that always makes me a little nervous, but after checking in with the funeral director, and getting a very necessary hot cup of coffee, I went back outside to find that Kurt Shaffer had decided to brave the elements on his Harley, and was present, with an Air Force flag flying. Kurt and I stood on the far side of the parking lot, where the sunshine and a break from the wind was making for an almost pleasant morning, awaiting the remainder of the crowd, but as it got closer to flag line time, it became apparent that we were it.

Let me make one clarification here, I had called Pam and Paul when I was setting up this mission and asked them to be my flag wagon, and they had graciously consented. However, when I realized that the weather was not going to be conducive to riding the Black Shadow, I had called them, and told them they could have the day off, as I would bring my flags. As it turned out, Paul was at Georgia National Cemetery for Mack's mission, but I didn't want anyone to think that they had neglected to show up for my mission.

Anyway, that being said, Kurt and I took positions on either side of the entrance, which was under the front portico, and thus in the shade, and exposed to the wind, and it was COLD! About fifteen minutes in, I had to go to the truck and get my gloves, as my hands were starting to go numb. PGR member Jim West rode in from Marietta around 10:30, and joined us on the flag line till 11 am. We broke down the flag line, had a short meeting with the funeral director and the hearse driver, and I left Jim and Kurt warming up in the kitchen area of the funeral home, with their directions on the escort, and I left for Georgia National Cemetery, to be certain that things were in order there.

But I had nothing to worry about. George (Sr. Chief) Westbrook had things in order, as he always does, and there was little for me to do but sit back and relax. The procession from the Funeral Home arrived just a few minutes after George had taken a large delegation of PGR members down to shelter #1 to set up, and Kurt and Jim were in perfect formation as they pulled in at the Information Bldg.

After checking with them on how things went, and commending them on a job well done, I joined the flag line at shelter #1, where the procession arrived some 10 mins later, with Kurt and Jim again leading the hearse in perfect formation. Sr. Chief called everyone to attention, as the casket was carried in. The priest spoke, prayed, spoke and prayed again. The Air Force honor guard stepped forward and raised the flag as Sr Chief again barked out orders, and "Bugler" James Brannon did another perfect rendition of 'Taps'. The flag is folded, the Air Force Sargent kneels and presents it to the widow of John Thomas Michael Collins, steps back, salutes, smartly turns and marches out. Our own Gracie then presented a PGR plaque on behalf of the Patriot Guard, and as she walks away, the flag line slow dissolves and retreats up the hill. 18 flag holders stood in what could be described as "less than ideal conditions" and honored the service of one who stood for us. Another mission complete, another mission "well done" by some of the finest Patriots I know, and I am honored to be able to stand beside them. I wish I could name every one of them, but I would forget someone, and offend by omission, but they know who they are. Thank you, each and every one, you honored a hero today.

Respectfully submitted,

David (wild1) Shreckengost

Ga. Patriot Guard Ride Captain

Another year in the books, more Heroes honored, a few laughs, some tears, always some tears, but thru it all, the Patriot Guard Riders came, they stood, holding that beautiful flag that we love, they did what they had to do, and for those families who requested their presence, they made a difference. They let the families know that their Hero was important, that their service mattered, and that we grieved alongside them. We cannot ask them for more than that.

With Honor and Respect

CHAPTER SIX - 2013

IT WAS A BAD YEAR

The year 2012 ended on a somber note, as you will see in this next ride report. Losing one of our Law Enforcement personnel always hits close to home, I have some very close ties to Law Enforcement, and really appreciate those who stand on the "thin blue line".

Ride Report: Joe Griffin, USA, LEO Jan 5, 2013

The news report got my attention. An American police officer who had gone to Afghanistan to train the Afghan police had been shot and killed by a female Afghan police officer, inside a secured area. It was Christmas eve, 2012, and with all that was going on regarding the upcoming birthday celebration, it really did not stand out in my mind. Not until I got a phone call several days later, did it come back to me. The officer who had been shot, Joe Griffin, had not only served with the Newton County Sheriff's Dept, but he had also served in the United States Army. That was when it hit home. This was a Georgia boy, he was one of ours, it was time for the Patriot Guard to stand for a hero.

Monday, Dec. 31, 2012. New Year's Eve. When many people are making party plans, stocking up on food and drinks, and preparing to blow out the year, the dedicated men and women who make up the Georgia Patriot Guard Riders were making their way to the Delta cargo terminal at Atlanta's Hartsfield-Jackson International airport. There were probably a dozen bikes already there when we pulled in, the overcast day was warmer than average for the end of December, and forecasted rain was nowhere to be seen. Bikes continued to arrive in a steady stream, and as we assembled for our briefing, there were 32 bikes and 3 cages present.

Our flag line was set up, with flags provided by Connie and Larry Harbuck, stretching the length of the Delta complex, down to the lower entrance, awaiting the family's arrival, only to have the escorted convoy arrive thru the upper entrance. But, as we often do, the Patriot Guard adjusted on the fly, with Larry Klein bringing one end of the flag line back to the cargo area, and Al Reger adjusting the other side, so it looked like we had planned it that way. As the family exited their stretch limo, the Patriot Guard was called to 'attention' and 'present arms'. After the family was inside, almost all the flags were rolled up and stowed, except for six that kept a vigil adjacent the hearse.

After a number of minutes, the roll-up door where the hearse was parked slowly opened, and the Newton County Sheriff's Honor Guard stepped into view, bearing the flag draped coffin. All hands were called to 'attention' and 'present arms' by a Henry County motor officer. The Honor Guard slowly places the casket in the hearse, the door closes, "order arms" echoes across the concrete loading dock, and Patriot Guard riders take to their iron steeds, to escort Joe Griffin home for the last time.

The ride from Atlanta to Covington is flawless. The Clayton County Sheriff's Dept covered every intersection till we were out of their jurisdiction, then the Henry County motor officers took over, and Newton County Sheriff's Dept had our backs, and we arrived at the funeral home without incident.

Bikes are quickly parked, and the Patriot Guard again assembles in two rows adjacent the hearse. The Sheriff's Dept Honor Guard again does their duty, again the commands are barked out, the shuffle of feet, the door to the funeral home closes, "order arms", and this part of the mission is complete.

Saturday, Jan. 5, 2013 was another day of above average temperatures for January, and once again, the forecasted rain appeared to be holding off. Al Reger and Jim Gordon were already parking bikes when we arrived at the Wheeler Funeral Home in Covington. We had decided not to park bikes at the funeral home, as there would be no escort, and we didn't want the service to be disrupted by motorcycles leaving, so Al and Jim were busy making sure everyone got parked okay. Bill Dowden rolled up, and we immediately put up static flags along the entrance, and also adjacent to the two ladder trucks, one from Newton County, and one from Covington Fire Dept, that were making an arch at the front entrance, with a large flag hanging between the two ladders, just as they had done when we arrived on Dec. 31st.

We had barely finished putting the static flags up, when sirens announced that the family was arriving. We assembled as quickly as possible, and came to attention and saluted, as the family entered the funeral home. As we assembled for a quick briefing, Joe Griffins father came over to our group, and expressed his deep gratitude for our presence. He spoke for several minutes, even tell us about Joe buying him a motorcycle, and making him take the safety course before he would give him the keys.

That was a hard act to follow, to say the least. If we had ever questioned whether or not what we do matters to these families, there was no question after that. Also don't think there were many dry eyes after that, either.

Our flag line was a beautiful sight in the slightly chilly air, just enough breeze to make the flags move, and a ray of sunshine, here and there, to make the red, white, and blue look that much better. A steady stream of family, friends and law enforcement colleagues came to honor Joe, and as Al and I stepped inside the chapel, it was filled to capacity. RC David Blanton dismissed the flag line at 1500 hrs., as Al and I stayed, and Al presented the condolence book put together by Lou Costello, to Joe's widow, Renee, and then we departed.

Another mission completed; many many people contributed to the successful completion. No PGR mission is a one man show, and I've tried to recognize as many who contributed, but it would be impossible for me to name them all. Those who come, stand the flag line, and then depart, without any recognition, are the core of the Patriot Guard, and they are the ones who make it all possible. Thank you each and every one, I salute you.

Respectfully submitted

David (wild1) Shreckengost

Ride Captain, Georgia Patriot Guard

As often time happens in the Patriot Guard, the motors on the bikes have barely cooled off, and it's time to go again. But it is an honor to be asked to stand for these who "stood for us", and we try to make as many as we can. In a little over 11 years with the Patriot Guard, I've managed to make close to 600 missions, and there are many who have done a lot more than that.

Ride report - Donald Patterson, Madison, Ga Jan 6, 2013

On a day that started out as less than ideal, Patriot Guard riders from around the State of Georgia suited up and pointed their iron steeds towards the small town of Madison, nestled in the rolling hills of central Georgia, to honor a man most of them had never met. Donald Patterson was a true American patriot, who had served in the United States Air Force and the United States Army. His stint with the Army included two tours in Vietnam as a Ranger, a truly dedicated man.

I had chosen The River Store on Greensboro Hwy in Madison for a staging area, because I knew there was a good possibility that the Sugar Creek Baptist Church would still be going strong at 12 noon, and as I passed the church, en route to the staging area, it turned out I was right. But even as church services were going on, our own Bill Dowden (Waterboy) was setting up a beautiful static flag line, as he said it, "hammering in time with the shouting". Amen, Bill.

The back-parking area of the River Store was already crowded with bikes when I pulled up on four wheels, but when you've got Mystik K riding with you, Baylee, the dog is almost certain to have to come along, so we have to make concessions. Saw a lot of familiar faces, and some new ones as well. Bikes continued to arrive at a steady pace, and there were nineteen bikes present when we had our briefing.

At 1200 noon, four family escort bikes lead by David (Hound) Blanton and Mallory (Pops) Granitz, Catfish and Wildman (not to be confused with Wild1) rolled out and turned left on Hwy 278 for the short ride to the family home. The rest of us made the left turn onto Sugar Creek Church Rd, and then left again into the grass below the fellowship hall of Sugar Creek Baptist Church. Church services were just getting over, and some of the parishioners seemed to think they'd been 'invaded', but handshakes and hellos were exchanged, even as the flag line was setting up.

At approx. 12:35 pm, our escort bikes rolled up with the family cars, in perfect formation. Several more bikes had arrived in the meantime, and by the time the service began at 1 pm, there were 27 bikes and 35 flag holders, standing straight and proud. The Patriot Guard was called to attention and present arms as the family entered the church. The service begins, and the flag line melts in to groups of two or three, here and there, as we await the conclusion of the service.

As the church doors open, approx. 30 mins later, the Patriot Guard is again called to attention, and present arms, as the notes of taps are again heard in the cool Georgia air. The flag line is reformed, in such a way as to make a corridor thru the cemetery across the street from the church. As the congregation moves in unison, the flag line closes behind them, and as they arrive at the burial site, they are completely encircled. A graveside service of near record brevity, and the family is moving back toward the church. We hold the line until all have departed, and then we depart also. Handshakes and thank you's, and one by one, they ride off again. Patriots who have come, done their duty, paid their respects, and will come and do so again, the next time they are called. I thank you, each and every one. None of this is possible without you, you are the Patriot Guard.

Respectfully submitted,

David (Wild1) Shreckengost

Ride Captain,

Patriot Guard, Georgia

Too many times we hear, "I wish I had known about the Patriot Guard when Daddy, 'my brother', or my cousin, or my sister died". We have no advertising budget, there isn't an office building with our name on the door, there is no secretary answering the phone. The only two places you can be certain to find us is on the internet, or at the cemetery.

Edwin Hoertz, USN, WW II, Conyers/Canton GA, Feb. 15, 2013

Another member of the "greatest generation" has reported to his eternal duty station. Edwin Hoertz served as a CPO aboard the USS Oberon, and saw action in the Pacific, Atlantic and Mediterranean theaters. He is survived by his wife of 62 yrs., 3 children, 8 grandchildren and 10 great grandchildren.

At the time of his passing, his family was unaware of the Patriot Guard, and when they were informed of us, their request arrived on too short notice, and we were unable to honor this hero at the memorial service held on Jan. 18.

Now, however, we will have to honor of escorting this hero to his final resting place at Georgia National Cemetery in Canton. As Edwin Hoertz once stood for us, in the difficult days of WW II, it will now be our honor and privilege to stand for him.

STAGING - NLT 1100 hr., Friday, Feb. 15, 2013

Ingles Supermarket parking lot

3530 Honey Creek Commons (GA 20 and Honey Creek Rd)

Conyers, GA.

KSU - NLT 1115 hrs.- to family home nearby

ESCORT - KSU - 1130 hrs.

Family home in Conyers - GA. National Cemetery, Canton.

SERVICE 1400 hrs.

Georgia National Cemetery

Canton, GA

RCIC - David (wild1) Shreckengost

wild1handy@yahoo.com

Apparently, this is another Ride Report that slipped through the cracks, so I stole one from my good friend, Ranger Bill.

Ranger Bill Burgess _to_ Georgia PGR Friends and Supporters

February 16, 2013 ·

AFTER ACTION REPORTEDWIN HOERTZ*** On Friday February 15th we were proud to Escort a True American Hero to his final Resting Place at the Georgia National Cemetery in Canton Georgia. Chief Petty Officer Hoertz was a Veteran of the Atlantic, Mediterranean and Pacific Campaigns during WWII aboard the Attack Cargo Ship USS Oberon. Twenty-Six Motorcyclists representing the Patriot Guard and American Legion Riders Staged in Conyers GA. to Escort the Chief and his Family to the GNC. Rockdale County and Conyers PD provided Escort from the Families Home to Interstate 20. From that point along the I-20, I-285, I-75 and I-575, 75-mile-long corridor our blocking Escort was provided by the Patriot Guards own who did an absolutely fabulous job of protecting the Convoy during its two-hour trek through the horrendous Greater Atlanta area traffic. We arrived at the Georgia National Cemetery and were met by another 16 Patriot Guard Members and together formed a Flag line during the Ceremony. As the Family sat gathered for this Final Farewell a baby babbled throughout the liturgy. This sound brought joy to my heart showing us that as one soul made its final transition another has started its complicated journey through life. Each and every one of these Missions shares a special meaning to us and every one of them helps to share the comradery that makes us who we are. Thank You to the Patriot Guard and to the members of the Loganville, Conyers and Buford American Legion Riders for making that so.

Thank you, Ranger Bill, and the Legion Riders for your support. You are a valuable part of our mission, and your presence is always appreciated.

Sometimes, what you might classify as an easy mission, becomes something special, and that was certainly the case with this next one. Nothing like standing around at the world's busiest airport, just because it's the right thing to do.

Ride Report: Send-off of 210th MP Co

It started off with a simple request, and turned into one of the most enjoyable missions we've done in a while. The request came from our fellow Patriot Guard Riders in North Carolina. Some of their soldiers, with the 210th MP Company out of Franklin, NC. were deploying to Afghanistan, and would be leaving out of the Atlanta International Airport, and would it be possible to have a flag-line at the airport to send them off.

It was a short notice request, less than 24 hrs., but with the dedicated members we have in the Georgia PGR, it was very possible. After talking to the Family Resource Officer for the 210th, my next call was to Connie and Larry Harbuck. Can you be at Atlanta airport at 8 am tomorrow with flags? And of course, they said yes, as they almost always do. I got the mission information posted on the Ga thread, then put a notice on Facebook, for people to check the Ga thread. Then took the Black Shadow to Columbus to stand in honor for SFC Richard Patterson, then on to the Blackhorse Manor, hoping that we would have a good showing for our MP's as they departed.

A good showing it was. 12 bikes and associated biker types hanging out at the far end of the South Terminal attracted several people's attention on a beautiful May morning. The MP's were scheduled to arrive at 0830, and when my phone rang about 0815 and the Sgt Major said, "We're stuck in traffic", I had to say that I was not surprised. No one said a word about the delay, everyone just 'hung out', flags at the ready, and spent the next hour just enjoying conversation and having a really enjoyable time of fellowship, as well as talking to several people about why we were there. Atlanta Police Officer Abrahams stayed with us, making sure that nobody bothered us, and we appreciated his assistance.

The Sgt Major had promised to call me when they got to the airport, and he did, just as their bus was rolling to a stop, opposite our position. We quickly formed up the flag line on both sides of the entrance. It took them a few minutes to grab all their gear, and make their way across the concourse. We gave them a round of applause as they made their way inside, and it was gratifying to see their expressions, the smiles on their faces, as they marched off into an uncertain future, knowing that their service was recognized and appreciated.

Just that quick, it was all over. Our soldiers were inside the terminal, getting their flight information, we rolled up flags, shook hands, hugged, and departed, with the knowledge that we'd helped in some small way to make these soldiers feel a little better about their mission.

Respectfully submitted

David (Wild1) Shreckengost

It was a real 'feel good' mission, sending those MP's off like that. Unfortunately, the next one was not a 'feel good' mission. As has been previously stated, Law Enforcement personnel are near and dear to my heart, and on lose one hurts, it just hurts, deep inside.

As a Ride Captain, you like the mission that are real straight forward, all you have to do is show up. Not a lot of 'moving parts' as we like to say. But even the most basic missions can have significant meaning for the families involved. We have another saying that we use often, "No matter how many missions you've done, for this family, it's their first". It is good to remember that.

Re: Ride Report, MSgt Howard Kenneth Genthner, Sept 1, 2013

On a beautiful late summer morning that started with just a touch of chill in the air, a dedicated band of patriots made their way to the National Cemetery at Andersonville Ga. An American hero had passed and it was their purpose to show honor and respect for his service to our country, and that is exactly what they did.

They came from near and far, Jonesboro, Jackson, Columbus, Phenix City Al, Thomasville, The Rock, Warner Robins, Crawford, and even a little town called Leary. There were other things that they needed to do, some took time off from their jobs, some left family and friends, but all with one purpose. Honor and respect.

Fourteen Patriots stood holding American flags in front of the shelter at Andersonville when the family of MSgt. Howard Kenneth Genthner arrived. The flag of the United States Air Force was closest to the walkway where the family passed, held by Air Force veteran and PGR Rider, Jerry Rape, who was standing the flag line along with his wife. There was just enough breeze to give the flags some life, and the quickly warming sun shone brightly down on the red, white, and blue.

MSgt. Genthner had raised a large family, and it appeared that all of them had made the trip to Andersonville to pay their final respect, along with many friends, the shelter area where his body lay was packed to standing room only. The Air Force Honor Guard rendered honors with all the precision and dignity that one could ask for. The flag folding, the three volleys that rang out in the summer air, the notes of taps, the flag is presented to his wife of 61 years, and the Honor Guard marches offstage.

Some words from a family friend, several minutes of memories from family members, and the service is drawn to a close. The flag line moves to the rear of the shelter area, and once again, honors are rendered as the casket is returned to the hearse for transport to graveside. As flags are being rolled and stowed away, MSgt Genthners daughter, Kenniane and her husband came down to our staging area, and thanked us for being there. Its simple gestures like that which really remind us of why we do what we do.

It was an honor to be able to stand for this man, who stood for us for 22 years.

Respectfully submitted,
David (Wild1) Shreckengost
Ride Captain, Patriot Guard Riders

Sending our soldiers off is always a difficult task. These men and women are leaving their homes and families to go stand for us, in an undisclosed location, usually overseas, and it was truly an honor for us to be able to send them off with our thanks and our prayers for their safe return.

Ride Report: Sendoff of 48th Infantry Brigade, Combat Team Dec 1 2013

On a day when they truly could have been anywhere else, 20 Patriots made their way to the Macon Coliseum to honor the service of the 48th Infantry Brigade, Combat Team, and send them on their way to Afghanistan with smiles and the knowledge that someone cares. It was still cold and dark when most of these Patriots pulled themselves from their warm beds, donned the necessary layers of clothing, mounted their trusty steel horses and headed off into the morning air.

The parking lot at the Macon Coliseum was already bustling with activity as they began to arrive, as almost 200 of Georgia's finest were assembling. They came from Greensboro, Waleska, Kennesaw, Douglasville, Jonesboro, Jackson, Macon and other cities. Singly, or in pairs, or small groups, they came, with only one objective. Show the men and women of the 48th Infantry that their service and sacrifice does not go unnoticed, and that there are those who care.

As the families, friends and soldiers assembled inside Hall A in the coliseum, they were quietly surrounded by Patriot Guard Riders, who lined the outside walls with flags, forming a symbolic ring of protection around those assembled. It was a large room and our numbers were small by comparison, but the flag line did not go unnoticed, and many a soldier shook many a hand, and their gratitude for our presence was very obvious.

Departure ceremonies follow a pretty standard protocol, and this one was no different. The colors were presented, the chaplain opened with prayer, numerous dignitaries expressed their gratitude for the service of those assembled, Gen. Butterworth spoke, the colors are retired, the Command Sargent Major dismisses the soldiers for their final hugs with family members as the flag line quietly exits.

Even as flags are being stowed, our heroes are boarding their assigned buses, our LEO's are lined up. Motorcycles are pulled into line, with flags waving, a thumbs up from the Sargent Major, blue lights come on, sirens sound, and we are underway. Thru Macon without a hitch, thanks to good work by the Macon Police Dept, and our Ga. State Patrol. About 7 miles out, we crest a small rise, and come to a halt in the road, and we are quickly informed that one of the buses has 'died'. However, it apparently was not a serious malady, as within a few minutes we were rolling again. A tip of the hat is also due the Macon - Bibb County Fire Dept, who had a truck accompany us to the county line, and at each fire station, engines were lit up, and crews standing at attention, in a well-deserved tribute.

Almost two hours, and almost 100 miles after leaving Macon, we arrived in Columbus, where the Columbus Police Dept jumped into action, getting us smoothly thru intersections and safely into the parking lot at Ryan's, where we got to share lunch with these fine soldiers before saying our final farewells. It was truly a unique and wonderful experience that none of us will soon forget

As with any mission we do, there are a number of different people who make it a success. Capt. Abby Walker did all the heavy lifting on this one, she is on top of her game. "Pops" Granitz was the initial contact, and asked me to take the lead, as he wasn't completely comfortable with his new ride captain hat yet. JR and Patty for bringing the flags, Sgt Holloway and Major, from the Ga. State Patrol did a great job of getting everyone to Columbus safely. But all that would not have meant a thing if it hadn't been for the flag holders that came, some had ridden more than 2 hrs., one had come down the day before, they are the ones who made this all possible, and they did an awesome job. Thank you all, the 48th got a wonderful send off.

Let's remember these brave men and women in our prayers every day, and when they return, make plans to be there to welcome them home.

Respectfully submitted,

David (Wild1) Shreckengost

Ride Captain, Ga Patriot Guard Riders

Another year is closed out, we've buried veterans, and law enforcement officers. We've sent some off to 'God only knows where' to stand in the gap for us, and we are grateful that they will step forward, and put their lives on the line. God bless each and every one of them.

CHAPTER SEVEN - 2014

IT WAS A DIFFERENT KIND OF YEAR

Sometimes, it just doesn't seem like the timing on mission request works out for you, but then sometimes, the missions just seem to come in bunches, and you go from not being the Ride Captain for any missions, to doing several at the same time, but as we always say, "you do what you can do, nobody can do them all". Then there are the missions that will remain etched in your mind forever.

Ride Report - Officer Kevin Jordan, USA, LEO June 8 – 9, 2014

Sunday, June 1, dawned bright and sunny at the SW Ga hideout. Up early as always, with coffee in hand, sat down at the computer to catch up on the world. Almost immediately the headline flashed across the screen, "Griffin Police Officer gunned down". My heart sank as the details seemed to blur together. Waffle House, extra job, unruly customer, shot in the back, it all seemed almost unreal. Officer Kevin Dorian Jordan, age 43, a husband, a father to seven children, a brother, veteran, and so much more. Cut down by a coward from behind while trying to protect and serve.

Several PGR members are familiar with officers in the Griffin PD, and word went out to them that the Patriot Guard was ready to stand for this fallen officer, should the family request it. About noon Monday, word came from Griffin PD that Officer Jordan's family wanted the Patriot Guard to participate, and it was our honor to do so. It quickly became apparent that despite the best efforts of Joe (Mack) McGuigan and Lt. Pike of the Griffin PD, the Patriot Guard was not going to be a part of the funeral procession, and in the end, it was probably better that way. On Friday, June 6, I met with Capt. Britt of Griffin PD at the cemetery, and we walked thru parking locations, graveside locations, and numerous other details that sometimes get lost in translation while trying to conduct everything by telephone.

Sunday, June 8th, was another bright sunny day, in Williamson Ga. The Oak Hill Baptist Church was a sight to behold as riders arrived in mid-afternoon for Officer Jordan's visitation. The church has put up almost 200 American flags, and they were absolutely brilliant in the afternoon Georgia sun. They were not actually put up for Officer Jordan's services, they had been put up prior to Memorial Day, and we were informed that they would be up until after the Fourth of July. How ironic that Officer Jordan's services had so tragically coincided with the church's expression of patriotism.

There were already several bikes at the church when I arrived, along with our own Bill Dowden, who, thankfully, did not have to set any static flags, as the church had already done a magnificent job of that. Bikes continued to arrive until almost all of the parking area that had been marked off by Dennis Scott, President of Southside Riders Association, was filled up. Dennis and a very sizeable contingent of Southside Riders were present to support the Patriot Guard and their support was greatly appreciated.

We had staged at the far end of the church parking lot, because there was a large, open pavilion there, and we had a four-hour visitation ahead of us, so we needed some place to rest and get shade. Word came from one of the funeral directors that the procession bringing Officer Jordan to the church would pass directly in front of our location, so when we heard sirens approaching, a flag line was quickly set up in front of the entrance where we were told Officer Jordan's motorcade would come into the church.

As so often happens, someone didn't get the message, and the entire procession entered the church from the other direction, which left us standing a flag line approx. 100 yds from where Officer Jordan's casket would be carried into the church. Nevertheless, when the hearse door opened, all present were called to "Attention", and when the flag-draped coffin slid slowly into the sunlight, "Present Arms" rang out, and we rendered honors, if only from a distance.

A quick briefing followed, and it was decided the Southside Riders would stand the flag line for the first 'shift', and the Patriot Guard would relieve them on the half-hour. We kept this schedule thru the four hours of visitation, some folks had to leave, others arrived to take their places, but the flag line remained in place for four hours.

Monday, June 9, 2014 is a day that will remain in the memories of all who were present at Oak Hill Baptist Church and at Westwood Cemetery for a long time. It was hot, with rain showers predicted, but thankfully, none appeared. Again, motorcycles lined the far end of the parking lot, and again, the Southside Riders showed up in force. Their participation on both days was a real asset, and contributed greatly to the success of the mission.

A short briefing, and our flag holders filed down, to stand behind uniformed officers at both sides of the church entrance. Many of these officers had been standing there almost since the start of our briefing, and one of the memories of that day was the sight of our own, Allen (Rocky) Watson, wearing shorts since he had caged to the mission out of fear of rain, carrying bottles of water to some very grateful law enforcement officers.

Again, sirens sound in the distance, getting closer and closer, and the family of Officer Jordan arrives for the last time. After the family has entered, "B" shift, Officer Jordan's shift, is called to 'attention', 'right face', 'forward, march', and they enter the church. The remainder of the Griffin officers file in behind them, followed by honor guards from more counties and cities than I could begin to count. Police officers from as far as Chicago came to Williamson Georgia, to say a final farewell to a brother that they had never met.

Once all the officers have entered the church, and the doors have closed, our flag line quickly makes for the welcome shade of the pavilion, where we divide up into three groups, each one leaving separately to go to the cemetery. Once we arrive, there is little to do but wait. Two large Fire Dept ladder trucks are out front of the Funeral Home, adjacent to the cemetery, and they are hoisting a large American flag, which is shining like a diamond in the afternoon sun.

Meanwhile, we located some horses on the other side of the funeral home, which requires further investigation. North Carolina Highway Patrol has sent four horses and a caisson to carry Officer Jordan, "the last mile". Although, due to the heat, it had now been determined that the transfer would take place directly under the large flag suspended from the ladder trucks in front of the funeral home.

Word comes that the service at the church is over, and the procession to the cemetery is underway. We can track to progress by watching the news helicopters, which are hovering above. When it becomes obvious that they are getting near, we leave the welcome shade trees, and trudge back into the hot sun, to the other side of the funeral home, where Mr. Bill is awaiting with flags, and more cold water. Even as the flag line is making its way across the grassy cemetery, police motorcycles begin to appear, coming up the rise from Airport Rd. Under the big flag, and filling up both side of the road, they form a solid line from one end of the cemetery to the other. Officers dismount, and stand by their machines, and wait. And wait. And wait. The Griffin PD's cars have filled up the cemetery behind us, other police vehicles are parking at the funeral home, across the street, where ever they can find a place, and they keep coming, and they continue to come.

Finally, the end of the procession arrives. Officers file into the cemetery and fall into ranks, with the Griffin officers of "B" shift closest to the gravesite. The flag line had to be adjusted several times to accommodate in influx of law enforcement officers. The caisson slowly makes its way down the slight slope, led by the Ga State Patrol bagpiper. It comes to a halt, and the Georgia State Patrol Honor

Guard gently carries Officer Jordan to his final resting place. We are too far away, and there are too many people to see what is taking place, but when the Masons leave, we knew things were drawing to a close. The Honor Guard steps forward, lifts the flag from the casket, and step back out from under the tent. Commands are given, seven shots ring out, and then again, and a final volley. The bugler lifts his horn, and the mournful notes of 'taps' seem to hang in the muggy evening air.

The flag is presented to his widow by the Chief of Police, a rose from the VFW, and three shell casings from the Honor Guard. There is a pause, then the roar of engines in the sky, five police helicopters make the fly-over, in a 'missing man' formation. Another pause, as the helicopters fade into the distance, then a radio crackles, "Dispatch to 3507", silence, "Dispatch to 3507", again, silence. By the time dispatch has finished 'the last call' there is not a dry eye to be found.

Capt. Britt escorted me up to Officer Jordan's widow, and I was honored to present her with a condolence book, and then turned around and presented a second book to the Chief of Police. I didn't tarry there; it was too hard to see. The flag line was already fading away, flags still radiant in the evening light.

It was a long two days, and an emotional ceremony at the graveside, but it was well worth it. Special Thanks to Dennis Scott and the Southside Riders Association, they were magnificent. Bill Dowden, with water and flags both days, was invaluable, couldn't have done it without him. Pam Long, for bringing flags and water and the beautiful condolences books, great job, girl. Well done. Mack, Laru, Jimdawg, Red K, Wordsmith, JayDub, Bees, Boots, Sibley, you all pitched in, made this thing work, thank you all so much. Hollywood, Cool Stick, Rocky, great job as always with the new people that turned out. It was truly a team effort, and one that was greatly appreciated by everyone that was there.

Respectfully submitted

David (Wild 1) Shreckengost

Ride Captain

Patriot Guard, Georgia

Honor Flight missions are one of the most enjoyable things that we do in the Patriot Guard. You have to get up real early, and we stay up till late at night, or early the next morning, but you leave that mission with a warm feeling, thankful for the men and women who have given so much for our freedom.

Ride Report: Honor Flight, Conyers 09-17-2014

Sometimes, it seems like the easiest missions that you do as a Ride Captain, are the ones you weren't planning on doing. Honor Flight missions in Conyers have been the exclusive domain of our own Larry (Laru) Klein, and this one was not expected to be any different.

But as we all know, in the Patriot Guard, expect the unexpected (Semper Gumby) and that's exactly what happened. Through a combination of circumstances, Laru was not able to RC this Honor Flight mission, and so it fell in my lap. Fortunately, Laru had done all the heavy lifting, all I had to do was show up. Amazing how difficult it is to go to sleep, knowing you've got to get up at 3:15 am, and you're scared to death that the alarm on your phone won't work for some unexplained reason.

But when I arrived at the American Legion in Conyers somewhere around 3:30 am, there were already three bikes waiting, and I had seen three more at the gas station across the street, so we were in good shape already. They continued to arrive in the darkness, one or two at a time, until 16 bikes were lined up, ready to go. A short briefing was made even shorter by the arrival of the Rockdale County Sheriffs truck which carries the wheelchairs for the Honor Flight veterans, so we scrambled to help them get the chairs loaded and ready to go.

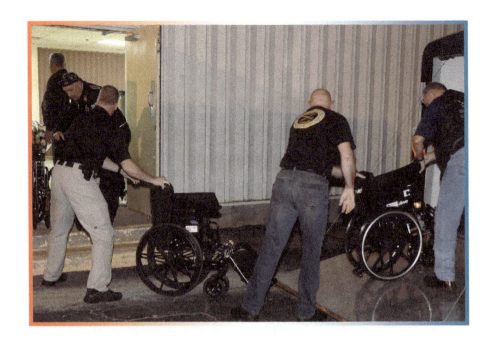

Then it was time to mingle, and this is what makes Honor Flight so much fun. We met a B-17 tail gunner with a funny story about flak jackets. A P-51 fighter pilot who was in training and landed in Pearl Harbor, en route to Okinawa on the day that the atomic bomb was dropped. These veterans are special, and they each have a story to tell, and getting to listen to them, is like stepping back in time. All too soon we have to head for the door and mount up, it's time to roll.

Our escort down to Atlanta airport was quite uneventful, thanks to the excellent work by the Rockdale County Sheriffs Dept, and the Georgia State Patrol, assisted by one officer from the City of Decatur. They do a great job, and Sheriff Levett and Rockdale County are to be commended for their dedication to helping the Honor Flight program. My hats off to them.

The International terminal at Atlanta's' Hartsfield Jackson Airport is still cloaked in darkness as we ascend the ramp, and park, amidst a sea of blue lights. All "non-essential" items are stowed away, the wheelchairs are unloaded, and inside we go. Our Delta representative met us there, and unlike some previous flights on another airline, the boarding passes we had requested were ready, and in her hands. Once thru security, (don't take you shoes off, BEEP BEEP Take your shoes off) we made one right turn, walked about 100 ft, and Boom, you're at the gate. Thank you, Delta, we didn't have to take the train, or walk to the far end of the furthest concourse, as we have had to do with other airlines.

Then it was time for more stories, taking pictures, and admiring the beautiful sunrise thru the east-facing windows of the International terminal. Finally comes the boarding call, and we line up to shake hands and wish these heroes safety for the journey. The last veteran and guardian disappear down the gangway, and the Patriot Guard makes for the exit. It's time for breakfast, that's how we roll.

The evening arrival at the airport is a little different then the morning send off. Four bikes rode in from Rockdale with the Sheriffs Dept, and I pulled up to the International terminal just as they were rolling to a stop. Several more bikes arrived at various times and stages, some decided to 'tour' the airport before arriving safely. Then the wait was on, finally a text message from our favorite paramedic, " On the ground". Then some more waiting, then here they come. More handshakes, "Welcome home', "have a good trip", a group photo, and then we had to carry on a tradition that Laru started, as we all sang "God bless America". The smiles on the faces of these heroes from days gone by, make it all worthwhile.

Everyone heads for the busses, and after a short delay to track down a missing wheelchair, the thunder of motorcycle engines and the sea of blue lights moves down the ramp and onto the expressway. Rockdale County and the Georgia State Patrol again to an excellent job of getting us safely back to the American Legion in Conyers. Park the bikes, unload the wheelchairs, help everyone inside for a brief ceremony, where our very own James Brannon, who had ridden all the way up from Warner Robbins, closed the evening with a perfect rendition of "Taps", on his horn that had been transported from Marietta by RC Nancy (Red K) Hitchings. Some final handshakes, and good-byes, and the Patriot Guard is headed to IHOP. That's just how we roll.

Thank you, Laru, for taking care of all the details, it was an honor to be able to stand in for you, hopefully, you'll be able to RC the next one. It was a long day, but worth every second. Thank you to all who came out, both early morning, and what turned into a very late night, may God bless you abundantly.

Respectfully submitted,

David (Wild1) Shreckengost

Ride Captain

Patriot Guard Riders

It's always tough to say good-bye to troops that are departing for parts unknown, it's a lot more fun to be able to welcome them home

Ride Report: 48th ICBT Homecoming 09-18-2014

I suppose you could say that it started last December. I had the honor of leading the Patriot Guard as we escorted the 48th Infantry, Combat Brigade Team, Georgia National Guard, as they deployed overseas. I got to know several members of the unit as we organized and planned, and the last thing we told them was, "We'll be here when you come home".

On a beautiful warm September afternoon, The Patriot Guard fulfilled that promise. 16 bikes and one cage assembled at the Museum of Aviation in Warner Robbins. After our usual briefing, we headed north to rendezvous with LEO from Bibb/Macon, only to discover that they had been delayed due to an accident enroute. Once they arrived, it was only a few minutes till word came that the buses were coming out the gate.

The escort back to the armory in Macon was handled very professionally by Capt. Walker and the officers from Bibb County Sheriffs Dept. One elementary school we passed had all the kids standing out front, with little American flags, that was an uplifting sight. Once we arrived at the armory, we dismounted quickly, and tried to shake as many hands as possible, as the troops left the busses, wishing each of them a hearty "Welcome home", and "Thank you". Many of them also thanked us for being there, and I reminded them that we had told them we'd be there, and it was obvious that they were very grateful.

The company is assembled, they march to the lower parking area where their families are waiting. The colors are presented, a few words from the commander, and they are dismissed. A very happy group of

Patriot Guard Riders slowly walked back to their bikes, stowed their flags, said their good byes, and rode off into the afternoon sun, secure in the knowledge that they had done good.

Respectfully submitted,
David (Wild1) Shreckengost
Ride Captain, Patriot Guard Riders

Most of the missions we undertake are one or two days, three at the most. This next mission consumed most of my time and energy for almost two months. Not your standard mission, fortunately, this one did not involve a funeral home or a cemetery. Construction work is not a normal method of operation for the Patriot Guard Riders, but when a veteran who has served our country has a need, the Patriot Guard steps up, and does what they can. We have as part of our mission, what we call Help on the Home Front, or HOTH, for short.

Help on The Home Front:

The Patriot Guard has an unusual opportunity to come to the aid of a Marine Vietnam Veteran in a different way. This mission is not so much about physical service, as it is financial assistance. Let me explain:

Danny and Lillie Mae live just down the street from us, as in David (Wild1) Shreckengost, and Kay (Mystic K) Tinney. Their house is badly in need of some repairs, and they are not capable of doing the work themselves, or paying someone else to do. Believing that "charity begins at home", or at least in your home town, we are trying to raise funds to help them out, and also looking for volunteers with some construction skills.

Replacing just the roof, which is really the most pressing issue right now, will cost approx. $1,600. We have volunteers lining up to help with labor, but if some of our Patriot Guard friends could help financially, that would be most appreciated. We have raised almost $800 so far, so we're making progress. You can view our Facebook page at: Help for a Marine in SW Ga, just type it in your search box on Facebook. If you don't like PayPal you can mail a check, payable to Kay Tinney, PO Box XXX, Leary, Ga 39862.

We hope to have all materials on hand by late Sept, or early Oct, and schedule a work day, get a bunch of people together, and get the roof part of this project knocked out in one day. There is also rotted wood and framing issues that need to be dealt with, but the roof is the top priority.

RCIC - David (Wild1) Shreckengost

678-663-2835

wild1handy@yahoo.com

We've set up a donate button on PayPal, and here is the link:

Phase One of this project was putting a new roof on the house. There was water running down the wall in the bedroom every time it rained.

HOTH – Help for a Marine Veteran in SW Ga 10-22-2014

I didn't think a 'ride report' would be appropriate for this mission, since no one showed up on a motorcycle, but people did show up, and a lot of work got done. When you're a Ride Captain, (although I'm not sure that would apply to this mission) you always wonder how many people are going to show up. When you've got a stack of shingles, multiple rolls of felt paper, and a Marine veteran with expectations, you really start sweating. Then you look down at your phone and see you have three missed calls from Poppa Joe, and you know things are going your way.

Saturday, Oct. 11, dawned bright and clear, with just a hint of fall in the air. Almost a dozen hard workers had assembled at 0800 hrs., and the day kicked off with sausage and biscuits, courtesy of Kay's mom, along with coffee and orange juice. A short briefing, and introducing those present to Danny and Lillie Mae Harrell, a word of prayer and work got under way. Poppa Joe and Mark Peeples from Gillionville Baptist Church started ripping fascia boards and rotted porch boards off the front of the house. Kenneth Sizemore and his crew from Sizemore House Repairs, started stripping shingles off the front of the house, PGR rider David Campbell from Bainbridge, and contractor Frank Fleming, from Athens, Ga were also hard at work. Rotted boards were ripped off and replaced, then felt paper rolled out. Drip edge gets nailed on, snap some chalk lines, and before lunch time, shingles are going on the roof.

Lunch was catered in by the ladies of the Leary United Methodist Church, and were welcomed by all. The sun and the gnats made the work slow down a bit after lunch, but by 5 pm, the shingles were complete on the front and side of the house, and the back had felt paper and was dried in.

We lost most of the work crew, as they had other things to attend to, so David and Frank headed for the local BBQ joint for some intestinal fortification, then got back at it, and had about half the back of the house shingled before dark.

Sunday, Oct. 12 was another beautiful day, and although it's not something I like to do, we had a roof to finish, so Frank and I got started as soon as it was practical, and with some help from Miss Kay, we had finished the shingles and had all the ridge vent and caps on before church let out.

Saturday, the 18th, was another beautiful day, and we were back at it. Epic Eric came over from Albany, and with his help, we stripped all the old shingles from the front of the carport, replaced all the rotted boards, and got it shingled before 3pm.

Sunday, the 19th, after church, we met a reporter from WALB in Albany, as they wanted to see what we were doing. After talking to them, it was home to change clothes, then strip the shingles off the back of the carport. Again, replacing rotted boards, even had to send Miss Kay and her mom to Albany to get some more, but before dark, the felt paper was down.

Epic Eric was back again on Monday morning, and we were back at it. Fascia boards were installed, then it was back on the roof, and shingles away.

Things moved along smoothly, and we wrapped up the roof about 1:30 pm. With cleaning up and loading up tools, it was well after 2 pm before we were done, done, but it was done.

Next work day is scheduled for Saturday, Nov. 8. At that time, we want to finish to soffit, replace some rotted wood, remove some old windows and replace them with new vinyl double hung, energy efficient windows. Would also like to install vinyl siding on the house. Obviously, this is going to take some manpower and materials, so if you can help with either, it would be greatly appreciated. We still have Challenge Coins for sale, $10 ea., if anyone is interested. Our Facebook page is "Help for a Marine Veteran in SW Ga", and there is information there if anyone would like to donate.

Please keep us in your thoughts and prayers as we try to help this Marine Veteran.

Respectfully submitted

David (Wild1) Shreckengost

Getting a new roof on this house was a major improvement, but the Patriot Guard was not through with this project, not by a long shot.

Ride Report HOTH mission 'Help for a Marine Veteran in SW GA', Phase two 11-10-2014

AFTER ACTION REPORT: PHASE TWO

Phase two of our renovation project on the home of Marine Veteran Danny Harrell and his wife, Lillie Mae, kicked off at 0800 hrs. on Sat. Nov. 8, with coffee, orange juice and pastries provided by Kays (Mystik K) mom, Bernice. Also present beside myself was Trish Jones, a friend of the Harrell's. Not a big crew for the work that needed to be done, but this is the Patriot Guard, we do what we can with whoever shows up.

Started work inside, removing drywall around the large window in the living room, and found even more termite damage than we had anticipated. Removed as much of the damaged wood as was possible, and re-framed the walls with new material, which Lowes in Albany had been gracious enough to sell to us at cost, which has saved us almost $1,000 on this project already. With new framing in place, new drywall was nailed up and by lunch time, the inside of the living room was looking almost new again.

Lunch was provided by Donna Wilkerson, who has been very faithful in feeding us on this project, and we are thankful to her for her faithfulness in that regard. After lunch we started working outside, and found that attaching the supports for the vinyl soffit to the hard board siding was not an easy task, even using pneumatic fasteners. Numerous adjustments of fastener types, and air pressure finally developed a method that would work, and before the day was over, the new soffit was in place all along the front of the house. In the meantime, Bernice and Trish had gone to Albany and purchased new curtains to replace the old broken blinds that had been removed from the living room window. These were installed with new curtain rods, to the approval of all present. If you were to drive past the house, you would probably only see the new window curtains, but progress has been made. There is still a great deal more work to do, and we hope to schedule another work day prior to Thanksgiving, so stay tuned, we need more help, regardless of your skill level.

Respectfully submitted,
David (Wild1) Shreckengost
Ride Captain, Patriot Guard Riders

Even as we are knee-deep in this home repair project, in addition to our regular job, missions keep coming, and we try to handle as many as we can. Our friends for the 48th Infantry again invited the Patriot Guard to welcome some of their folks back home, and once again, the Patriot Guard was happy to oblige.

Ride Report, 48th IBCT Welcome Home/ Ribbon cutting 11-10-2014

On a beautiful late fall morning, 6 patriots on motorcycles and one flag wagon (flag corvette?) made their way to Macon to, as Rodney Blitch put it, "finish a mission we started a year ago". It was indeed, Dec 1, 2013 when the Patriot Guard stood a flag line as members of the 48th Infantry, Combat Brigade Team said goodbye to their family and friends and departed Macon for Iraq and Kuwait. On Sept. 16 of this year, the Patriot Guard was again present to escort our returning heroes from Warner Robbins AFB to their HQ in Macon.

On Friday, Nov. 8, the mission was completed, as the 48th held their official 'homecoming' ceremony, and also had the 'official' ribbon cutting for their new HQ's building. It was our honor to be present, and to be able to report that the 48th suffered no casualties on their deployment, for which we are extremely grateful.

Thanks, and a high five to David (Hound) Blanton, who did all the hard lifting on this one. Bruce Tamker, whose flag corvette definitely lends a little extra class to our missions in middle Georgia. George Patton, Mark, Eric, Rodney, thank you guys, your dedication is greatly appreciated.

Respectfully submitted,
David (Wild1) Shreckengost
Ride Captain, Patriot Guard Riders

Another mission found its way onto the schedule in late November, and this one is one we still talk about to this day.

Ride Report – USN Lawrence T. Dorn, 24 Nov. 2014

Most of the time, when we as members of the Patriot Guard Riders attend the funeral of a fallen serviceman, or a veteran, or first responder, you are immediately aware of the impact your presence has made. I've held widows and wives who were crying, received hugs and handshakes from fathers and friends, and when you put your bike in gear, and ride away from there, you know in your heart that you and all those who stood with you have made a difference in someone's life.

When the Combat Vets Motorcycle Association contacted us regarding honoring the life and service of Lawrence T. Dorn, USN, Vietnam veteran, we were told that he had no family, and had not the Combat Vets intervened, he would have been buried in a pauper's grave. As a young man, Lawrence Dorn stepped forward, raised his right hand, and put his life on the line for our freedom, and the Patriot Guard was going to be present to honor his service, and let everyone know that he was not forgotten.

On a beautifully sunny November Monday morning, 18 patriots came from across Georgia to Andersonville National Cemetery to let the world know that every veteran matters. They were Patriot Guard Riders, American Legion Riders, Combat Veterans, but all joined as one in honor and respect.

We had assembled behind the pavilion at Andersonville when the hearse carrying Lawrence arrived. We rendered honors, and then became pallbearers, wheeling his casket to the place of honor at the front of the platform. As we got our flags out, and started to line up in front of the pavilion, a school bus from Carrollton Ga pulled up out front, and a large group of students disembarked, and came up the side walk beside our flag line and onto the platform. I thought to myself that this was a bit odd, but the Ranger in charge seemed to know what she was doing, so a group of high school students, on a field trip to Andersonville, had the honor of being part of Lawrence 's final farewell.

I don't know what was going through their minds, but when the brief service was over, I hope they had at least learned something. The service was quite brief, a few words to the students from the funeral director, then the familiarly haunting notes of 'Taps' from the Navy honor guard. The flag was folded, and presented to the teacher in charge, the honor guard marches off. We held our flag line as the students departed, and rendered honors again as the casket is wheeled away.

The flag line retreats, flags are rolled up, stowed away. Handshakes, hugs, and good-byes are said, "see you next time" is a familiar phrase, because we know that there will be a "next time", because freedoms defenders deserve honor and respect, even those who have no 'family' to stand for them. The Patriot Guard Riders made Lawrence T. Dorn part of the family, and he shall remain part of us, forever.

Respectfully submitted,
David (Wild1) Shreckengost
Ride Captain, Patriot Guard Riders

Then it was back to work on our 'project'.

HOTH – Help for a Marine Veteran in SW Ga 12/7/2014

Just wanted to give everyone an update on where we stand on this mission. On Friday, Nov.28, Patriot Guard Riders Harry Traywick, Jimmy Revell, Jerry Green and myself changed out all the windows on the home, and installed new, energy-efficient vinyl double hung windows. We got house wrap and siding on the garage side of the house, and most of the front of the house.

On Sat, Nov 29, Commander Ray Humphery from the Sylvester American Legion came with one of his guys, and a grill. They worked hard, and cooked well, and we got the siding on the front and the right side of the house finished.

On Sat, Dec 6, the Sylvester American Legion post was back in force, with Ray, Muddy, Michael, Cody, Mark and his wife, and two of Ray's granddaughters. We finished the siding on the front gable, side gable and the rear of the house, so all of the siding is now done. They also finished all but about 4 ft of soffit on the back of the house, and wow, what a difference.

We did have one little hiccup with the electrical system, but Mark Peeples, an electrician who attends Gillionville Baptist Church in Albany, came out this afternoon, and got that straightened out.

We still have soffit to finish on the carport, windows to trim, inside and out, drywall to repair, and some painting to do inside. With that thought in mind, we have scheduled another work day for Saturday, Dec. 20. I really appreciate the Sylvester American Legion for doing all the heavy lifting on the last two work days. They have really done a great job, and we are so appreciative.

With that being said, would love to see some more Patriot Guard Riders on Sat, the 20th. Would love to have a big group show up, and just blitz this house out, and be done with it. We'll feed you, and even put you up overnight if needed. Jerry (Crawdaddy) Green came all the way from Dallas and spent two nights at the SW Ga hideout, and he survived. So, come on down, bring hand tools, and a stepladder if you have one, and let's get this thing knocked out before Christmas. What an awesome Christmas present that would be.

Sincerely

David (Wild1) Shreckengost

Ride Captain

Patriot Guard Riders

HEADS UP, PATRIOTS:

Work day - Help for a Marine Veteran in SW Ga. Sat. Dec 20, 0800

We're looking to finish up this project before Christmas, so come on down.

Need to finish the soffit, some window trim, inside and out, painting window trim outside, drywall repairs, and interior painting, all needs to be done before Christmas.

Wouldn't that be an awesome Christmas present for Danny and Lillie Mae?

So come on down, we'll feed you, and even put you up for the night. Bring hand tools and a step ladder if you have one. See you Sat, Dec. 20, 0800

Unfortunately, Saturday, December 20, was a washout, as cold winter rains prevented us from doing any work that day. With the Christmas holidays, and New Year's coming up it was not until January 2, 2015, that we were able to resume work on this home.

HOTH – Help for a Marine Veteran in SW Ga, Jan 2, 2015

Started work at 0800 hrs. on Friday, Jan 2, with just myself and my nephew Brian Spiller, a contractor from South Dayton, NY, who had driven down on New Year's Day, to give his uncle a hand, and it was much appreciated. We started working on the soffit and fascia around the carport, and were hard at work when PGR members Jimmy Revell, from Moultrie Ga, and his son Jason arrived. They dove right in, and by lunch time they had siding up on the gable end of the carport and almost all the soffit and fascia completed.

After lunch, I cut trim pieces for the interior of the new windows, while Jimmy and Jason nailed them in, and Brian finished up a few exterior trim items. After a trip to Albany for more materials, we tackled the rotted wood under the large windows in the front of the house, and that turned out to be a task. But with a little persistence and some persuasion, we were able to get new wood under the window, and new trim underneath, and it was time to wrap it up for the day. A very productive day, and a tip of the hat to Brian, Jimmy and Jason, they all did a great job.

Saturday, Jan 3, was gloomy and gray, with rain threatening, so Brian and I started priming and painting the exterior window trim, hoping to get it done before rain set in. Mark Peeples, from my church, Gillionville Baptist in Albany arrived around 9 am, to deal with some electrical issues. He made short work of those (no pun intended) then grabbed a paint brush and painted the fascia around the entire house before he had to leave. I finished putting the final coat of paint on the window trim, even as Brian was running new trim in the Living room, and prepping it for painting. By the time I was done, he had a coat of primer on the ceiling and was priming the drywall that he had coated in the Living Room. I helped him move furniture and stuff around so we could get to the walls and started putting on the final coat, thinking that we were going to wrap this thing up.

I couldn't have been more wrong. As we started painting the outside walls in the Living room, large pieces of old paint and drywall began to peel off, onto the paint roller, some falling on the floor. A combination of termite and water damage, it brought us to a screeching halt. To say that I was disappointed would be the understatement of the year.

So, now we'll have to scrape the outside walls, removing any loose material, skim coat them with drywall mud, let that dry, sand, prime and paint. WORK DAY, SATURDAY JAN 10, YA'LL COME ON DOWN!!

I'm going to do the scraping and drywall work on Friday, Jan, 9, so we're going to need painters on Saturday. Lots of painters. Bring rollers, brushes roller pans, short extension handles if you have them, and let's get this project finished with a BANG! We'll feed you, even put you up for the night if we need to. We're this close to being done, people, let's do this.

Respectfully submitted

David (Wild1) Shreckengost

I can truthfully say that I was never happier to have a mission (or project) behind me than I was this one.

As of 1507 hrs., 1/10/15 - It is my honor to report: Mission Complete.

All the interior painting has been finished, walls and trim in Living room, and one hallway, which was all that we were asked to do. Still have some leftover pieces of siding, and trash to haul away, which I will do either tomorrow afternoon or Monday, but we have done considerably more than what was originally envisioned.

PGR members Jimmy Revell and his son Jason came from Moultrie, Ray Humphrey, Commander of the American Legion post in Sylvester was here today, and we got it done.

A full after-action report will follow in a day or two.

David Shreckengost

Ride Captain

Patriot Guard Riders

If a full after-action report was written, it got lost in the shuffle somewhere, and it's probably just as well. We tried to recognize everyone who contributed to this project as we went along, and they have my undying and eternal thanks. I still drive by Danny and Lillie Mae's house at least once a week, and it's still one of the best-looking houses in Leary, Ga.

It was a busy year, but a very rewarding one. One of the perks of this job.

CHAPTER EIGHT — 2015

CLOSER TO HOME

By this time, in the State of Georgia, the Patriot Guard was organized in such a way that Ride Captains were no longer running all over the state to do missions. It meant that the rides to the missions were sometimes shorter than in days past, but the mission is still as meaningful, both for us and for the families that we serve.

Ride Report - Samuel P. Seay 04-12-2015

It started with a phone call, and when it's a fellow PGR member on the other end of the line, asking if you'll do a mission for another PGR members family, you can't say no.

Samuel P. Seay was one of those men you wish you'd had a chance to sit down and talk with, because there was obviously something extraordinary in this man. Sgt. Seay served 11 months in the jungles of Southeast Asia, and in that short period he was awarded four Bronze stars for valor in combat. This man was truly something special, and I'm certain that he will be greatly missed by those who had the privilege of knowing him.

The weather didn't look all that great when most of us rolled out of bed on an April Saturday, but by the time it was kickstand stands up, the sun was starting to make its appearance, and the ride up to the church in Jonesboro just got better and better, despite having to make a detour to pick up a hat for our newest SW mentor, Jerry Rape, and then having to dodge I – 75 traffic, and take the back roads.

Arrived at the church just before noon to find Bill Dowden and Larry Klein already busy putting up static flags. The layout of the church just lent itself to a static flag line, and what a beautiful sight it was. I didn't count each one, but there had to have been close to 50 static flags. Across the edge of the street, down both sides of the driveway, in both flower beds at the front entrance, and along the walkway. A truly impressive sight, and a beautiful reminder that a hero was being laid to rest.

Bikes and cages began to roll in, as the dedicated members of the Patriot Guard Riders came to do what they do best, show honor and respect to those who have served our country. One bike, another, several more, they came steadily, until 21 patriots had assembled. Considering that we had four other PGR missions on this day, and one 'Fallen Hero" ride in N. Ga, this was a pretty impressive turnout.

We had a short briefing, and I introduced our newest SW Ga mentor, Jerry Rape, and presented him with his official blue hat, with his ride name on it. While the briefing was ongoing, our PGR brother Bobby Wiggins arrived with Samuel's family. Bobby's wife was Samuel's sister, and Bobby was the reason the family requested our presence. I almost didn't recognize Bobby with a suit on.

With the briefing finished, we took advantage of what shade we could find, as the sun had begun to make it feel more like August than April. The flag line went up shortly before 1 pm, and remained until just a few minutes prior to the start of the service, when we stashed the flags and lined up at the entrance in column of two.

We entered the church, directly behind the family, and paused at the door to the sanctuary, as the minister welcomed everyone and had his opening prayer. Once he said 'amen', the command 'forward' was given, and we marched down the center isle and stopped at the first row of pews. Larry 'Laru' Klein presented the condolence book to Samuels' daughter, Kim, and then we lined up across the front of the church, rendered honors, and then marched back up the isle and out of the church.

Flags are rolled up, static flags stacked, and more rolling. Rebar on the right, beside the wheel well. Flags in, feet first. Handshakes, and more handshakes, 'thank you', hugs, 'be safe', 'see you next time', as we walk away, knowing once again, for just a minute or two, the Patriot Guard made a difference, helped someone to know that their loved one was not forgotten, that their service was appreciated, honored, respected.

It's just what we do.

Respectfully submitted,
David (Wild1) Shreckengost
Ride Captain, Patriot Guard Riders

The following report is rather brief, but if I had put in it all the stories we heard about Carl Beck, it would have been twenty pages long. To say that he had a distinguished career would be an understatement.

Ride Report - MSG(Ret) Carl Beck 09-19-2015

On a beautiful late summers' day in Ga, when you felt like God was smiling down, 13 Patriot Guard and American Legion Riders came together to honor a man who truly was an American Hero.

We had the honor of standing a flag line for this man, but more than that, we got to know something of him, and his many experiences during WW II.

We talked to his friends, one of whom had served with him in the 501st Parachute Reg, and stood alongside us, carrying the Regimental flag, as Carl's body was moved from the Education building at Clairmont Presbyterian Church, where he had been lying in state, to the main sanctuary.

We rendered honors, both at the church and at the cemetery, later that afternoon, yet we felt like we were honored to be present to pay final respects to this departed warrior. It was truly one of the most memorable missions that I've ever done, and the stories and legends of Carl Beck will continue to be told for many years to come.

Thank you, Sir, for your service to our country.

Rest in peace, Soldier, your mission here is complete.

Respectfully submitted

David (Wild1) Shreckengost

Ride Captain

Patriot Guard Riders

Most of the missions we undertake are called "Honor Missions", in which we are asked to honor someone who has passed away, be they a veteran, active duty military, first responder, etc. Only two of these missions have ever moved me to the point that it was felt to be necessary to write two Ride Reports. This is one of those.

Ride Report- SrA Kcey Ruiz, USAF, KIA, - Part one 10-13-2015

A day that dawned wet and dreary had turned to beautiful autumn blue skies as 37 bikes and two cages assembled on very short notice at Tara Field in Hampton. It was a day of honor and respect, as Senior Airman Kcey Ruiz, age 21, came home for the last time. Patriot Guard Riders, American Legion Riders, Southside Riders, Combat Vets and others, all there for one purpose.

At 1338, the small white charter jet touched down on the runway, as more than 40 American flags waved gently in the autumn breeze. The removal of the casket, the precise steps of the Air Force Honor Guard, commands barked into the stillness, a familiar drama to most that were there, but one that still touches their heart. This is why we do what we do. Honor, earned in a far-away land, respect, knowing that we owe her more than we could ever repay. It is truly why we wear dark glasses, as tears are a common sight up and down the flag line.

The hearse starts to move, escort bikes fall into place, and the procession is underway. Small displays of respect all along the way. Every vehicle is stopped, some standing with hands over their hearts, veterans hold their salute until all have passed. Thru Griffin, where flags and salutes are seen in abundance, even as we rolled down Ga 16 to Jackson, every intersection held those who wanted to pay their respects to a fallen hero. Over I-75, and heading into Jackson, where it seems that every person in town has come out to line the streets.

Flags, signs, Fire Dept ladder trucks with large flag hanging over the road, it was simply awesome. Small town Georgia turned out, most of them, like most of us, wanting to honor a hero that they had never met, yet knowing in their hearts that it was the right thing to do.

Two more turns, into the parking lot, off the bike, and across the yard to the funeral home, where the Patriot Guard Riders who escorted the hearse, are now helping to carry its precious cargo inside. Render honors, once again. The door closes, and Kcey has come home for the final time.

Handshakes, hugs, pats on the back, "Well done", "see you next time", and they slowly drift away. Some have far to go, others not so far, but all have a home to go to in safety, because brave men, and women, like Kcey Ruiz, stepped forward, raised their hand, and laid their lives on the line for us. We truly are in their debt.

Respectfully submitted

David (Wild 1) Shreckengost

This one was real close to home. From what I call my 'second home' at the Blackhorse Manor in Jackson Ga, it took approx. 5 mins to get to the church, and even today, as I pass that church, I can still see the hearse, the motorcycles, the Air Force personnel lined up, reminders that 'freedom is not free'.

Final Ride Report – SrA Kcey Ruiz, October 16, 2015

The Patriot Guard Riders came to a small town in central Georgia, on a beautiful fall day, a day that started chilly, and ended the same way. Blue skies, a pleasant breeze, the type of day that a lovely 21 yr. old girl should have been strolling through the leaves without a care in the world. But this 21 yr. old, this very special girl, with the sparkling eyes, and the beautiful smile, this girl had given everything she had for the cause of freedom, and on this day, this beautiful early fall day in Georgia, the Patriot Guard had gathered to pay their final respects to this girl, and to escort her to her final resting place.

Airman 1st Class Kcey Ruiz, posthumously promoted to Senior Airman, had a desire to serve her country and her fellow man. Her dedication to duty was beyond question, and her commitment to freedom lead her to a distant land called Afghanistan, and there she gave her life, so that we might continue to live ours as free men and women, and for that we are forever in her debt.

To put into words all the events of this day is far beyond my power, but to say that it was a day that shall live in our memories for many, many, years, would be a good starting point. From putting out static flags at the church in the early morning light, hearing sirens and the rumble of motorcycle engines and the hearse carries this special girl to the church for the last time. The many Air Force personnel both enlisted and officers, the myriad of law enforcement officers, legion riders, many others, and all assembled for one purpose.

The family arrival, to procession into the church, the music begins to play, inside mourning, outside waiting. Service over, call to attention, render honors. On your bikes, and we're rolling out of town. Speed up, slow down, police bikes from one jurisdiction pull off, to be replaced by others. Traffic, and more traffic, finally we've arrived.

Down the hill, Shelter # 1, flag line already in place, Air Force Honor Guard already in place. Everyone waiting, waiting to say their final goodbyes, to honor their fallen comrade. The Honor Guard, so straight, erect, precise, the family, packed in, tears, sobs, a prayer, a volley, then another, and a third. Taps, what a mournful tune, flag folded, presented to a grieving mother, father and sister, by a 2-star general. A condolence book, courtesy of the Patriot Guard, and it's over. Kcey Ruiz will be forever 21.

It was a long ride home after that mission.

The next mission was also close to home, to my 'first' home. It's only about 23 miles to the Funeral home where the visitation took place, and Andersonville National Cemetery is only about 60 miles from my house, which is a real short distance for a Patriot Guard mission.

Ride report - GySgt James Hinman, USMC 11-18-2015

On a very warm November Tuesday evening, 10 Patriot Guard and American Legion Riders assembled at an Albany funeral home, in silent honor and respect for a man who was described by one who knew him well as " a Marines Marine". James Hinman had survived the Battles of Iwo Jima, Guam, and the "Frozen" Chosin Reservoir in Korea, and had a chest full of medals. It was truly an honor that his family had requested our presence, and they were very appreciative. Friends and family, coming to pay their respects, thanked us again and again, and told us how much they appreciated what we do. It was a very pleasant flag line, and the time passed quickly.

Wednesday, Nov. 18, dawned gray and cloudy, with rain threatening to break loose at any minute, but once again, the Patriot Guard and the American Legion assembled at the National Cemetery in Andersonville to pay their final respects. Hugs and handshakes all around, a short briefing, the Pledge, and a prayer, and the flag line falls into place along the walkway. Just a few short minutes, and the hearse emerges behind the flag pole, slowly circles, and makes its way down the hill, and around behind the pavilion, where a very sharp looking Marine Honor Guard awaits. The limousine and the family cars pull up at the circular drive in front of us, and we render honors as they make their way up to say farewell to their hero.

As the last family member passes, the flag line wheels to the right, and forms up in front of the platform. A few words from the minister, almost inaudible at this distance, then two Marines step forward. They salute the flag draped coffin then gently lift and hold the flag. Behind us, the Commander of the firing party is barking orders, the command "Fire", and seven rifles shatter the afternoon stillness. Again, and once more, a full 21-gun salute for "a Marines Marine".

"Present Arms", and salutes are rendered. As the bugler raises her instrument, a light rain begins to fall, almost as if Heaven itself is mourning the loss of this Marine. The last note sounds, "Order arms", hands come down, at ease. The flag is folded, presented to his daughter and the Marines step smartly from the platform. The funeral directors roll the barren casket away, and it's over. The flag line slow fades away, knowing in their hearts that today, we did a good thing, today, for a few minutes, we made a difference for one family. It's why we do what we do.

Respectfully submitted,
David (Wild1) Shreckengost
Ride Captain, Patriot Guard Riders

As has been previously stated, the Patriot Guard Riders manage to find themselves in some unusual situations at times, but this was the first time for us to pull up to a residence, and there is a sign that says, "Thank you, Patriot Guard, for bringing Poppa home". That just made my day.

Ride report, William Jackson, USA, 21 Nov. 2015

To say that every mission we undertake is different and unique would certainly not be an understatement, but the "last ride home" for William Jackson is definitely one that those who participated in will not soon forget.

Saturday, Nov. 21st dawned cloudy and cold, and it was time to drag out the cold weather riding gear. It was definitely the coldest riding since February, but the Patriot Guard Riders didn't let the temperature keep them from doing the right thing.

Fifteen bikes and one cager (who was recovering from a slight accident on his previous mission) made a welcome sight as they assembled in Hapeville. A weeks' worth of trying to line up LEO support had been less than fruitful, so our very own Otto (Amsterdam) Ojevarr, professional escorter was a welcome sight. He did an excellent job of getting us to our destination safely, and we are most grateful.

Mr. Jackson's remains were picked up at Atlanta Mortuary Services, and safely stowed away as Darryl (Big Dog) Gunter called the Patriot Guard to "Attention", and "Present Arms".

With Otto running interference, and Big Dog leading, the procession made its way safely onto I - 285, then north to I - 20, and the eastward turn toward home for Mr. Jackson. Rockdale County Sheriffs Dept picked us up at their county line, and as we passed Salem Rd, they shut down the interstate, and Bill Jackson had it all to himself, that was very cool.

Newton County picked up the escort at the top of the ramp at Almond Rd, and had all the intersections covered till we got to the sub-division, where we learned not to follow the Sheriffs Dept too much, but it all worked out.

As we drove past the Jackson home, there was a substantial crowd of people waiting for his arrival. Bill (Waterboy) Dowden had set up a static flag line to honor Mr. Jackson, and it was a beautiful sight.

We rode past the house, down the end of the cul-de-sac, circle around and park on the road in front, with Mr. Jackson's ashes being on the only motorcycle in the driveway. The Ga Army National Guard Honors Team carried his remains inside, and Mrs. Jackson insisted that we all join her as she wanted to tell us some stories about her husband.

Cramming 16 bikers and all the family and friends into a not so large house was rather amusing, but we made it. Mrs. Jackson told us how proud her husband was of his service, and the more she spoke, the more you wished you had gotten to know him.

When she was thru, the Honor Guard stepped in, and we had to move back so they could have some room. The flag was brought out, and then thru the open front door came the bugle notes we've all heard many times, but the notes that still stir our souls. Taps is played, salutes are rendered, then, the flag is unfolded, and folded again, in a space that wasn't large enough to fold a flag, but the Honor Guard pulled it off without missing a beat. The flag is then presented to Victoria, and the Honor Guard marches out, job well done.

With the memorial service complete, Mrs. Jackson insist that it's time to eat. As we go into her kitchen, it appears that she has enough food to feed an entire division. There is even a cake that says "Thank you, Patriot Guard" on it. That is definitely a first. Everyone did their best to pack away as much food as possible, but Mrs. Jackson was still wanting us to take some with us when we left.

It was a most unusual mission, but one that we walked away from with a feeling of satisfaction. William Jackson was home. It was a good feeling.

Respectfully submitted

David (Wild1) Shreckengost

Ride Captain

Patriot Guard Riders

This was another one of those missions that was 'close to home'. It's nice not to have to ride three or four hours (or more) to honor a Hero. But we'll do it, if that's what it takes. Patriot Guard Riders are good like that.

Ride Report - Thomas David Preston, USN 12-06-2015

Those of us who have been involved in the Patriot Guard Riders for any length of time know that mission request come from all different directions, but when you roll out of bed at 0700 on a Saturday morning, you're not really thinking about trying to pull a mission together for that afternoon, but that's exactly what happened.

A quick check of the 'smart' phone while still only half awake, and there it is, a request for a Ride Captain to honor a Navy veteran, and it is less than 8 hrs. away, and it's in Albany, which is, figuratively, in my back yard. First thought is, "no way, too short of a notice, we've got the family coming this afternoon, the grandbabies will be here, just can't do it". Then the next thought is, "why not, Let's make it happen".

A phone call to the point of contact, which in this case was Patricia, his lovely wife of 34 years, and you learn why we do what we do.

Thomas David Preston was one of those guys who wanted to be where the action was, and he certainly got his wish. As a communications specialist aboard the USS Cimeron, he went ashore with the Marines

at Inchon as a Naval Artillery Spotter, which meant he was right in the thick of things.

Having assured Mrs. Preston that we would be there, the mission info is sent to National for posting, and then on to Facebook, everybody's friend. It's always good to have friends who know people, and Ray Humphrey, from the Sylvester American Legion Post 335 knows everyone who lives in SW Ga, and when Ray says he'll be there, and bring friends, that is exactly what happens.

11 Patriots showed up at Mathews Funeral Home in Albany on less than 8 hrs. notice, to stand for a man, who, many years before, in a faraway place called Korea, had stood for us. We were truly honored to be able to participate in this mission. His wife and family were very grateful for our presence, and the many visitors also expressed their gratitude.

Yes, we missed a few moments with the family, and the grand-kids, others gave up time with their families also, but for a few moments, the Patriot Guard Riders, and the American Legion Riders made a difference for one family that was mourning the loss of a true American Hero.

Rest in peace, Seaman, your mission here is complete.

Respectfully submitted,

David (Wild1) Shreckengost

Ride Captain

Patriot Guard Riders

It was a good 'extremely short notice' mission to close out the year. To be able to honor those who have sacrificed for us, some giving everything they had for our freedom, it is a humbling experience. We have a saying in the Patriot Guard, "If a man says he's never cried, he's never stood with the Patriot Guard Riders". We shed some tears, but that's okay. It's well worth it.

CHAPTER NINE - 2016

ANOTHER YEAR OF HONORING HEROES

The new year got off to a fast start, with another mission that was close to home. One of the things I love about living in Georgia is that, even in January, it's warm enough to throw a leg over, fire up the V-twin, and ride to honor another Hero.

Ride Report, CMSgt Winburn Willis 01-02-2016

To say that Edison Ga is a small town, is almost an insult to small towns, although it is larger than Leary, which is famous only as being the location of the SW Ga. hideout. When the mission request came in, for Chief Master Sergeant Winburn Willis, after I told Wordsmith that I would take the mission, my first thought was, who in the world is going to come to Edison?

Thankfully, patriotism knows no boundaries, and distance is often a 2nd thought when a hero needs to be honored. On a cold, crisp January morning, Patriot Guard Riders, and American Legion Riders from as far away as Macon, suited up, threw a leg over their iron steeds, and rode to SW Ga, because a man who had stood for us, now needs us to stand for his family, to let them know that we appreciated and honored his service to our country, and so they rode.

Thirteen bikes, two cages and eighteen flag holders made their way to the Edison Baptist Church. Many of them could have gone to other missions, that were closer to their homes. (Ga Patriot Guard Riders had six missions on Saturday, Jan 2, 2016) but they came to Edison, and the family was truly grateful. Mrs. Willis went down the flag line with tears in her eyes, and hugged everyone there, and told them how much she appreciated them being there. There is something special about being hugged by an 80'something year old lady, that touches you to your core, and you forget the cold, the ride over, the pain in your knees from standing, it makes it all worthwhile.

No mission goes exactly according to plan, and this one was no different. We were originally scheduled to escort the procession to the cemetery, but that got cancelled at the last minute, so when the service began, we quietly made our way to the cemetery, and had the flag line in place once again, when the procession arrived.

The Honor Guard themselves had made a little trip, coming out of Montgomery, Al, and they performed their duties flawlessly. The flag is folded, three volleys are fired, and those hauntingly familiar notes of taps sailed across the clear cool air of a small cemetery in SW Ga. A condolence book, graciously provided by our own Gen. George Patton, is presented, and the flag line quietly files away, knowing in their hearts that for one day, for one family, in a small town called Edison, in SW Ga, they have made a difference. No fame, no TV cameras, no newspaper coverage, just patriots doing the right thing.

No mission happens by itself, and if I may, a well-deserved tip of the cap to Ray Humphrey, and American Legion Post 335, for their outstanding support. Gen George Patton brought part of his posse from Macon, Bonaire, and Byron. Fort Gaines, Tifton and TyTy Ga were also represented. Epic Eric brought flags, and a sense of humor. All played a part in making this a mission that one family will remember for a long time.

Respectfully submitted

David (Wild1) Shreckengost

Ride Captain

Patriot Guard Riders, Georgia

Once again, the motors on the bikes had barely cooled down, when it was time to fire them up again, and ride over to the Marine Logistics Base in Albany, which once again is a short ride from the SW Ga. Hideout. This one was definitely a first for the Patriot Guard and Legion Riders, but it was a very moving mission. Read on.

Ride Report - Covella Pond Rededication - Marine Corps Logistics Base Albany 01-08-2016

Patriot Guard mission request come from all over, and you never know exactly what you are going to get into, when a request flashes up on your computer screen. When this request came in for a "Pond Re-dedication", my first thought was, "that's got to be a first". Then, when you dug a little deeper, and you got to know about GySgt. Joseph F. Covella, Sr., and learned the story behind this American Hero, Covella Pond took on a whole new significance.

GySgt. Joseph Franklin Covella, Sr. enlisted in the United States Marine Corp in 1947, as a reservist. His active duty date is 1950, when he got shipped to Korea, and won a Silver Star for leading his platoon up a hill. After Korea, he returned home, married a nice girl from the neighborhood, and raised five children, until the Marines sent him to a little-known place in SE Asia, called Vietnam.

There, while deployed with the South Vietnamese Army, the company he was with was ambushed. During a vicious firefight, the order came to withdraw. GySgt. Covella's platoon provided cover fire for the rest of the company to withdraw safely, then as they tried to retreat, three soldiers were wounded. GySgt. Covella stayed with the wounded, and provided cover fire for the rest of his platoon, and was killed as a result of his heroic actions, which resulted in another Silver Star, posthumously.

Covella Pond was named for GySgt. Covella in 1968, and is the most recognizable landmark at Marine Logistics Base Albany. It is a place where Marines work on fitness, and a place for families to assemble, and today, his widow, and four of his five children and their families, along with many friends, and fellow Marines, came to Covella Pond, fifty years after GySgt. Covella made his valiant sacrifice, to rededicate the ground that is named in his honor.
It was a gray, cool, foggy day, but that didn't stop eleven Patriot Guard and American Legion Riders from honoring this Hero. They escorted the Covella family from their quarters to the ceremony, and then formed a beautiful flag line that gave some much needed color to the gloomy January day.

An opening prayer, a reading of GySgt. Covella's Silver Star certificate by his daughter, brief remarks by the Base Commander, some family remembrances, the laying of two wreaths, one by the Marine Corps League, one by the family, and then those familiar notes of 'Taps' float out across the grey water of Covella Pond, to be answered by the echo of another bugler on the other side. Salutes are dropped as the last note fades away; the flag line withdraws quietly.

Flags are rolled up, stowed away, hugs, handshakes, "See you next time", because we know there will be a next time. As long as men like GySgt. Joseph F. Covella, Sr. stand for the cause of freedom, there will be a 'next time'. Covella Pond, a fitting tribute to a warrior, and a reminder to the rest of us that "freedom is not free".

A tip of the hat to the good folks at Malones Paint and Body Shop, who weren't certain what to think when bikers started showing up in their parking lot, but they welcomed us like long lost relatives. The ever-reliable George Patton and his sidekick, Lee Lacy came all the way from Macon. Ray Humphrey, and the American Legion Riders from Post 335 Sylvester, great turnout as always. Harry Trawick brought flags from Thomasville, and the mission wouldn't have been complete without them. All those who came, stood, and rode away without any applause or fanfare, I salute you all.

Rest in peace, GySgt. Covella. Your legacy lives on at Covella Pond.

Respectfully submitted,

David (Wild1) Shreckengost

Ride Captain

Patriot Guard Riders

Almost a month later, we got word that Riverdale Ga Police Major Gregory

"Lem" Barney had been gunned down while backing up his officers as they searched for a armed robbery suspect. Another mission that hit close to home. Too close.

Ride Report, Major Gregory E. "Lem" Barney 02-20-2016

I suppose you could title this one, "The mission that almost wasn't". Although the Patriot Guard Riders have been honoring America's fallen heroes for over ten years, there are still some people who are not aware that we don't simply "show up" at someone's funeral. Each and every mission we undertake is at the invitation of the family, or in the case of First Responders, (Police, Fire, EMT) an invitation from their department is sufficient.

When the news broke about the tragic death of Riverdale Police Major Gregory E. "Lem" Barney on 11 Feb, there were several attempts to reach out to the Riverdale Police Department, to make them aware that the Patriot Guard was ready to stand for this fallen Hero, and assist in honoring his service in any way possible. Unfortunately, a number of days went by without any response, a new family contact was passed along to us, and another message was left, and still, nothing but crickets.

As new media announcements detailed the funeral services for Major Barney, it began to appear that an invitation would not be forthcoming. However, on Thursday, Feb 18, with services scheduled for Saturday, Feb. 20th, one of our Mentors rode his motorcycle to a training class that was part of his job, and as fate would have, several deputies from the Clayton County Sheriff's Dept were also there, and when they saw the Patriot Guard patch on his vest, they asked him if the Guard was going to be at the funeral on Saturday. They seemed somewhat distressed when Danny explained to them that we had not received an invitation, and within 10 minutes, Danny had the contact numbers for the Honor Guard that was handling the funeral detail.

Danny passed that information up the chain, contact was made and by mid-day Thursday, we had an invitation, and profuse apologies for not contacting us sooner. However, because all of the arrangements for the church service and procession to the cemetery had already been completed, after meeting with the funeral director, all parties agreed that we could best honor Major Barney by providing a flag line at the cemetery, and late Thursday, we were finally able to alert our membership that we would be able to pay final respects to Major Barney.

They asked for flags, and flags is what they got. Approximately one hundred and twenty static flags were placed at the entrance to Forest Lawn Cemetery, lining both sides of the drive and providing some much need color to a cool and cloudy February day.

That many flags don't jump out and put themselves up, and all hands present participated. As there were other funerals taking place near the location of Major Barneys grave, we waited until those were complete, and then placed more static flags around the area where his service would be, providing a beautiful back drop to a somber event.

Waiting. We do a lot of it, and this Saturday was no exception. Rumors abound, and this day was no different. The North Carolina Highway Patrol had brought a team of horses and a caisson to carry Major Barney to his final resting place, and we had just finished putting out flags and had stopped by to admire the horses, when they got word that the funeral procession was 45 minutes away. Having talked extensively with the funeral director, and knowing what his projected schedule was, out came the smart phones, log on to the local tv station, and they are live streaming the service, so we know they won't be at the cemetery in 45 mins. Gotta love the internet. Waiting, we're back to waiting again.

Finally, we get confirmation that the procession is enroute, so we walked several hundred yards from our staging area to the gravesite, twenty dedicated Patriot Guard Riders, all of whom could have been anywhere else, but they chose to be here, in this resting place for heroes, because they understand the sacrifices made on their behalf, and this is how we honor and appreciate those who make those sacrifices.

Even while waiting, there are moments of sharing, and we were asked to take a group picture with the City of Atlanta Police Honor Guard, which got rather comical, trying to get everyone positioned for a good photo, and we got a chance to express our appreciation for the job that they do, and they returned the thanks as well.

Sirens are heard in the distance, and we know the procession is approaching. Line up, straight line, flags poles straight up, just enough breeze to make them stand out, and almost wish you'd put your jacket on. A steady stream of police and family vehicles, parking, doors slam, the funeral director and the Honor Guard Sergeant getting everyone lined up. More and more officers, recognized two from Chicago, some from New Jersey are directly in front of us. It takes almost a half-hour before everyone has taken their place. Then silence.

Silence. Then, from across the cemetery, the first wailing notes of a bagpipe, the piper comes into view, leading the magnificent black horses which pull the caisson on which the flag draped coffin rest.

The notes of the bagpipe, the clip clop of horses' feet on the pavement are the only sounds, as if the world has stood still for a moment to recognize a Hero is passing.

"Caisson, Halt", and the horses stop. The rider less horse, boots reversed in the stirrups, following the caisson is not so cooperative, and two City of Atlanta mounted officers have to keep him in check. The Honor Guard steps forward, commands ring out, all come to attention and salute as Major Barney is carried to his final resting place.

The minister speaks briefly, the flag is lifted and held aloft. Seven rifle shots pierce the silence, a second volley, then the third. As the hauntingly familiar notes of 'Taps' begin to sound, a few sprinkles fall from the skies. Angel tears? From behind us comes the unmistakable sound of rotors beating the air, and seven helicopters fly slowly over, in the missing man formation.

The flag is presented, doves are released, and suddenly, it's over.

"All uniformed personnel, DISMISSED". The flag line fades away, static flags are removed, rebar pulled, flags rolled up, stowed away.

"See you next time", because we know that there will be a next time.

As long as men like Major Gregory E. "Lem" Barney stand for us, there will be a time when we will need to stand for them. And, if invited, the Patriot Guard will be there.

A special tip of the hat to John 'Lonewolf' Hartman and Jimmy and Pat White for bringing the flags. John brought Bill Dowden's flags, as Bill could not attend. To all who came, helped, stood, and rode away, my most sincere "Thank You". You are the Patriot Guard Riders, and you make this all possible.

Respectfully submitted,

David (Wild1) Shreckengost

Ride Captain

Patriot Guard Riders

Repeat business is good for most businesses, in the Patriot Guard, we're really not looking for repeat business. But when one of my PGR brothers loses a veteran member of his family, how can we not go?

Ride Report - Thomas Cleveland Blitch 03-27-2016

As we all know, ride requests and missions come from many different directions. When I opened Facebook on Wednesday, March 23, and saw a picture of my friend, Rodney Blitch with his uncle Cleveland, and he said that his uncle had passed away, you just knew that this was going to be a Patriot Guard mission. The Blitch family believes very deeply in serving our country. Rodney can rattle off names, going back to his Great-grandfather, of those who have served in the armed forces, including three of his cousins currently on active duty.

We first met Rodney and the Blitch family five years ago, at a small brick front funeral home in Pembroke Ga, when his father, an Army veteran, passed away. Two years later, the Patriot Guard was back at the same funeral home to stand a flag line for his uncle Earl, and on a March Saturday that threatened rain all day, the Patriot Guard rode into the fruitcake capital of the world, Claxton, Georgia, to honor the service of another member of a family that has given so much to our country.

Eight bikes and eleven flag holders made their way to Claxton, to stand beside a Patriot Guard brother, and to honor his uncle, who had stood for us back during the time of the Vietnam war, when it was not popular to do so. We stood the flag line for two hrs. of visitation prior to the service, working in shifts, so no one had to stand the whole time.

Patriot Guard missions are known for spontaneous happenings, and this one was no different. The location of the funeral home made it an outstanding location for some static flags, and Leon (RiverRat) McLamb, and George (General) Patton took it upon themselves to procure the necessary supplies to make it happen. A tip of the old maroon cap to the one and only "Poppa Joe" Black for bringing the flags all the way from Valdosta. For a sexy senior citizen, he does get around.

We stand down the flag line when the service begins. Some gather and talk quietly, some grab lunch at a convenient restaurant. Poppa Joe heads over to the family pond, and is ready with flags when the Patriot Guard arrives, having escorted the cremains to that place.

We park quickly, grab flags and line both sides of the gate, as the family makes their way to a lovely pond, where Cleveland had spent many hours fishing, and where he had asked to have his ashes scattered. The family gathers round, the preacher has a few words, then prayer. Then to the surprise of most everyone there, two boxes of ashes are produced, those of Cleveland, and also Uncle Earl, who passed several years ago, they will now be forever together at the edge of a small pond in South Georgia.

The ashes are poured out together, as the Patriot Guard renders honors. The light breeze carries the scent of magnolia and wisteria as the flag line fades away. We gather around our brother, Rodney, amid hugs and tears, and once again, for a family that has given so much, for a few minutes, the Patriot Guard Riders were able to give a little something back.

Flags are rolled, hugs, handshakes, a slap on the back, "see you next time", because we know that there will be a next time, Lord willing. Motorcycles crank up, and move out, and this mission is complete.

Respectfully submitted

David (Wild1) Shreckengost

Ride Captain

Patriot Guard Riders

When you get a request from another PGR brother, asking if the Patriot Guard can come and stand for a friend of his, you assume that it's something that will take place within the next few days. But, not necessarily. You just never know.

RIDE REPORT - VICTOR A. LAMBERT - UNITED STATES ARMY 04-05-2016

Back in late February, received a text message from Patriot Guard Rider Rodney White, regarding a member of his Elks Lodge who had passed away. The Lodge was going to do a ceremony to remember him, and Rodney wanted to Patriot Guard to be there to stand for his brother Elk, and I assured him that we would do so.

Assuming it would be within the next week, I told Rodney that I was booked up, but that I would pass it along to Cricket, NW Ga Asst State Captain, since it was in her region, and she would be able to find a Ride Captain to handle it. Oh no, no, no, Rodney said. It won't be until the 5th of April. Okay, nothing on the schedule that far in advance. mission is on.

Victor A. Lambert graduated Marist High School in 1957, and then joined the United States Army, where he served three years on active duty as a photographer, and then did three additional years in the reserves. He returned to Atlanta, and as we learned at the very impressive Elks ceremony, had a very distinguished career both in television and theater in the Atlanta area.

It was a relatively straight forward mission. We would stand a flag line in front of the Lodge, prior to the Elks ceremony, and we would then accompany the guest to the Grand Ballroom, where we would occupy the end chairs on every other row, to honor Victor during the ceremony. As we all know, with every mission, life also happens. My flag wagon guy, Bill (Waterboy) Dowden's warehouse manager died suddenly with a massive heart-attack at age 49, so Bill had to run over to the Elks lodge and stash some flags, so he could attend his managers funeral.

Yours truly had some personal situations happening as well, and so I made sure the we had back up. John (Lonewolf) Hartman, and Jeremy (Shaggy) Shirah were both glad to step up and assist, and they did a great job of getting static flags set up, and the flag line in place, when the RC got caught in Atlanta afternoon traffic, and finally arrived 5 minutes late.

The Elks were most gracious host, and one after another took time to thank us for being there, and told us how much they appreciated it. As time drew near for the service to begin, we moved inside, to find that our plan to sit on the outside seats of alternate rows was not going to work, so we lined chairs across the back of the ballroom, and provided a beautiful red, white, and blue backdrop to a very interesting and moving Elks ceremony.

When they opened the floor to those who were friends of Vic to speak about him, we got a glimpse into the life of the man, and his influence on those around it, and it made the day even more special.

When the ceremony concluded, we stood our line until all the guest had departed, and then made our exit. We rolled up the flags, pulled the static flags, and stowed them in Bill's van. Bill had driven three hours from the service of his warehouse manager in Vidalia, to be present for Vic's service, and his dedication is duly noted.

We had been invited by the Elks to joint them in a luncheon, and most of us gladly accepted. "Gunny", and "Bud" had to roll, but the remaining riders enjoyed an excellent meal, and some good old-fashioned camaraderie around the table. Then it's time to roll, hugs, handshakes, "see you next time", because we know there will be a next time. This is the mission, it's what we do. "Standing for those who stood for us".

Respectfully submitted,
David (Wild1) Shreckengost
Ride Captain, Patriot Guard Riders

When you get a mission request, and it includes the words, "Delta Air Cargo, Hartsfield Jackson International Airport", you know it's not good. A servicemember has given everything they had for this country, and it's time to saddle up, and escort them home, with honor and respect. We don't get a lot of missions that cross state lines, but this one did, and it was a very special Memorial Day.

Ride report, Sgt. Michael Pellegrino USA, AD

Momma used to say, "If you don't want to do something, don't be checking your email at 11 pm." But sometimes we fail to heed momma's advice, and when you do, you discover that the Patriot Guard Riders have been asked to accompany an American soldier on his final journey.

Six years ago, Michael Pellegrino stepped forward, raised his right hand, and wrote that blank check for the amount of 'up to and including my life'. He will forever be 25 years old.

Saturday, May 28, 2016 will long stand in the memories of the patriots who made their way to the Delta Air Cargo facilities on International Blvd. The brisk morning ride in from the outskirts very quickly gave way to shirtsleeve weather as we stood alongside the Honor Guard at the top of the ramp, alongside a gleaming black hearse. 17 Patriots, all of whom had other plans, stood, erect, American flag in their left hand, honor and respect in their hearts.

Time seems to almost stand still as the flag draped coffin is brought up near the entrance, and his family gathers around, and the finality of the moment begins to set in. After a few moments they slowly walk away, wiping the tears. The Honor Guard moves forward in precise unison, their footsteps echoing through the facility, as all other operations at this busy building have come to a complete halt.

"Lift", "Forward", "Halt" "Center, Face"' and the casket slowly disappears from sight, as honors are rendered. Salute are dropped as the rear door closes and the flag line dissolves into a jumble of motorcycle and cages, lining up to begin this final journey. The CAO's van, carrying Michael's mother, is the last to get in line.

Follow the blue lights, as an APD cruiser leads the procession slowly down International Blvd, and safely onto the interstate. Then our own Sidecar Larry and Sid 'Squirrel' Kelly took over escort duties and safely saw this small procession to a rest and refuel stop in Madison and then on down I - 20 east, to Exit 1, North Augusta, where a goodly delegation of South Carolina Patriot Guard Riders was waiting.

Handshakes, introductions, hugs, and the Georgia portion of the mission is complete. A final hug for Michael's mom, and we roll west, carrying the knowledge that on this Memorial Day Saturday, there is nothing we could have done that was more important than this. Once again, for one family, for a few short moments, the Patriot Guard Riders have made a difference, and that's all that matters.

Respectfully submitted,
David (Wild1) Shreckengost
Ride Captain, Patriot Guard Riders

The back story to this mission is: coming back toward Jackson on I – 20, I was exiting the interstate in Covington when the clutch cable broke on my 2001 Victory V92c, affectionately known as the "Big Red Machine". Got in touch by phone with Larry (Laru) Klein, and he hitched up the trailer and came and got me off the side of the road. Not the ending that you want to have, but these things happen, and it's always nice to have friends.

CHAPTER TEN — 2017

THE BUSIEST YEAR YET

As has been mentioned before, mission request come at all times of the day and night, and sometimes it works out with your schedule, many times it does not. This particular year, there were a lot of missions that seemed to fit into my schedule.

Ride Report, Donald E. Sanders, USAF, 12 Jan 2017

Request for Patriot Guard missions come from many different sources, but when the brother of an Air Force veteran, who himself has ridden with the Patriot Guard, ask for us to come and stand for his brother, you can't say no.

Middle of the week missions, especially short notice ones, are always some of the hardest to get people to come out for, we all have life going on, plans, some of us even have to deal with that ugly thing called a J-O-B, and there were already two other missions on the board for the same day, so when you pull up at the funeral home at 1 o'clock in the afternoon, and there are already static flags being put out, and three bikes in the parking lot, and the service is at 3 pm, you know you're off to a good start.

Bikes continued to pull in, one after another, until 10 motorcycles and 12 flag holders were present and reporting for duty. It was a beautiful day in Middle Georgia, temp in the low 70's, felt more like April than mid-January. We held a short briefing prior to setting the flag line, and this one had a bit of a twist to it. We see things happen sometimes, and we call these "God winks". During the entire briefing, the flag in front of the funeral home had been hanging limply at half-mast in the afternoon sun. As the briefing concluded, and we turn to salute the flag, and say the Pledge of Allegiance, which we do at every mission, a gust of wind caught the red white and blue, and it stood straight out as 12 patriots rendered honors. Some would say, it's just a coincidence, but I've seen enough of these moments at PGR missions to know better.

12 Patriots standing proud, greeted those who arrived for the funeral service, and most if not all expressed their gratitude for us being there. At 3 pm, the flag line stands down, and all hands work at getting flags rolled up, put away, and then go remove the static flags so that Jimmy White, our flag wagon man of the day, can proceed to the cemetery and be prepared for the graveside service to follow.

At the conclusion of the service, all present rendered honors as the casket is carried out, and as it is loaded into the back of the hearse, Don's brother Ben, in his Army uniform is facing the hearse, with a perfect salute to his brother, and you didn't have to be a rocket scientist to know how difficult that had to have been.

We mount up, engines come to life, and we're pulling out, Henry County Sheriffs Dept doing an excellent job of getting us through some major intersections without a hitch. Into the cemetery, Jimmy is directing traffic, and we roll to a stop. Off the bike, grab a flag, get everybody together, and the flag like forms on the side of the hill, facing the burial site.

Family and friends gather round, the minister says a few words, has prayer, then steps aside. The Air Force Honor Guard steps in, raises the flag from the casket, step to the side, and fold it, calmly, quietly, with precision. Then one steps aside, walks a short distance down the hill, raises the shiny bugle, and those solemn, haunting notes of 'Taps' float over a sun-drenched Georgia cemetery, and you're reminded once again of why we wear dark glasses.

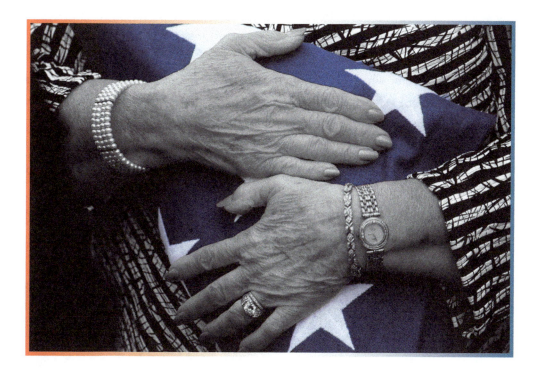

Service is over, the flag line makes its way down the hill, flags are rolled up and stowed away, again. Get the static flags, pull up the rebar, everything put away. The handshakes, hugs, pats on the back, "see you next time", "be careful riding home", and one by one, 12 Patriots go their way, with the knowledge in their hearts that for a few minutes on this spring-like winter day, they made a difference for one family. I am proud of each and every one of them.

Respectfully submitted

David (Wild1) Shreckengost

Ride Captain

Patriot Guard Riders

Weather is always a factor when a mission request come in, but almost without exception, the Patriot Guard Riders step up, regardless of the weather.

Ride Report – Roy Chester Maddox, USN. 4 April 2017

On a day when every weather forecaster in sight was predicting utter disaster to strike, eight American Patriots made their way to the Mt. Olive Baptist Church in McDonough to pay their final respects to retired US Navy veteran Roy Chester Maddox. Introductions are pretty easy when you have three David's and a Bill, so to add a little diversity to our lineup, four guys from Redeemed Biker Church came out for their first mission, and then we had a Donald, a Dale, a Reno, and Irish.

Despite the off and on showers, which sometimes seemed to be blowing sideways, the flag line came to attention as the hearse stopped in front of the church, and honors were rendered, as the flag draped coffin, complete with rain cover, was slowly rolled inside.

The flag line remained in place, adding some much-needed color to a very gloomy spring day, until the service began, and another downpour descended. A tip of the very wet ride captain's hat to Bill Dowden, who came down from Tucker to bring flags, and then got the privilege of taking some very wet flags back to his warehouse to dry out.

David Andrews, David Barton and yours truly rounded out the cast of characters, who refused to let a 'little' rain stop them from honoring an American Hero.

It was my humble honor to be able to stand beside them.

Respectfully submitted,

David (Wild1) Shreckengost

As has been previously mentioned, only two missions have ever caused me to write two ride reports, this is the second of those two missions.

Ride Report – Spc. Carl A. Trice, Part 1, June 2, 2017

Some Patriot Guard missions just seem to come out of nowhere sometimes, and this one would certainly fall into that category. On a Wednesday after work, I'm waiting out a brief shower so I can go out and cut the grass at the Blackhorse Manor, and the phone rings. And it all goes on from there.

Carl A. Trice, age 26, Specialist, United States Army, 82nd Airborne Division, on vacation, riding a motorcycle, like so many of us like to do. Car pulls out in front of him, and he will forever be 26 yrs. old.

Thirteen American Patriots made their way to Delta Cargo at Atlanta Hartsfield – Jackson International Airport on a picture perfect Friday afternoon, where we were joined by one new rider, GA Army National Guard Sergeant Gregg Sheed had gone to High School with Carl Trice, and when he heard the tragic news, Gregg knew he had to do something, so he rode from Columbus, Ga, to Atlanta, to help carry his friend home for the last time, and we were glad to welcome him into our Patriot Guard family.

As any Patriot Guard mission, there is always any number of things that can, and sometimes do, go wrong, but the angels were with us, both the winged version, and the ones on four wheels with blue lights, and we had both in abundance.

Getting law enforcement escorts for missions is sometimes harder than pulling teeth, but when you've built up a good list of contacts in many different jurisdictions, and, one of your riders is on the Honor Guard for the Clayton County Sheriff's Dept, and Clayton County is the first county we'll be traveling thru, well, you get the idea. I was expecting one or two cars, WRONG, we got twelve. There is nothing, absolutely nothing that makes a Ride Captain happier on a Friday afternoon, facing Atlanta traffic, than to have law enforcement vehicles lined up from one end of the parking lot to the other, and this is not a small parking lot.

Even as the last of the Clayton County Sheriff's cars are lining up, the familiar 'whoop, whoop" of police sirens tells us that the Upson County Sheriffs Dept has arrived with the hearse, and the family, and we are once again brought back to the task at hand. The flag line is quickly assembled, its members standing in the footsteps of where a flag line stood in this same spot just three days ago.

The hearse backs slow up the ramp, gets lined up, stops. The Honor Guard steps forward, they open the back door, and stand in formation, waiting. It's not a long wait, as the tug, towing the special trailer that Delta uses for these occasions, rolls to a stop just out of public view, in this immense facility. The Honor Guard snaps to attention, and moves with slow, precise steps into the building, returning momentarily with the flag-draped casket firmly in their grasp, as commands ring, out, and honor is given.

Salutes are held until the door closes, then it's roll up the flags, get on the bike, make sure Atlanta Police know what Clayton County is doing, and where Upson County is going to line up, and whose going out first, etc, etc. The one thing the Ride Captain forgot to mention to the LEO's is that flags on bikes tend to shred quickly at high speed, and we normally like to travel at a 45 – 50 mph pace. RIGHT! I won't forget to tell them next time.

We rolled out of the airport, Atlanta Police in the lead, Clayton County next, and the rest of us fall in behind. When we rolled down the ramp onto Interstate 75, all you could see was blue lights in the far-left land, making a path, and boy, did they ever. If you could have videotaped Clayton County Sheriffs Dept making a path thru Atlanta traffic, you could use it to teach a class. These guys were on it, and they had us thru the Friday afternoon backups like they didn't even exist.

But they weren't done yet. Knowing that Henry County Police Dept had only assigned two vehicles to assist us in getting through the bottleneck that is Henry County traffic on almost any afternoon, Clayton County stayed with us, and help Henry County PD get us thru traffic in record time. At one point, reaching 70 mph, which had me praying that no flags would come off, or flagpoles break.

Have to give a shout out, and major kudos to the Henry County Fire Dept. On very short notice, they had one of their snorkel trucks sitting on a bridge over the interstate, with a beautiful huge American flag hanging from the bucket. It's a sight that never gets old, and the family was very moved by this beautiful tribute.

The Good Lord was looking out for us, and having cleared the traffic bottlenecks on I – 75 South, we rolled smoothly thru Butts County, where only one Sheriffs car was sufficient, then off the interstate onto Hwy 36, where Lamar County had one unit to take the lead for us.

Thru Barnesville, at speeds much faster than what was posted on the signs, and headed toward Thomaston. Lamar County breaks off at the county line, and the Upson County boys are now on home turf and its hammer down, again. We picked up additional Upson County units as we went along, and City of Thomaston Police joined in also, so that when we hit the square in Thomaston, it was again awash with blue lights. Around the courthouse, left turn, down the hill on Highway 19, right turn past the cemetery, weave thru some back streets to the point that you're not certain you'll find your way back again, and then the left into the driveway of the small funeral home. Circle around, park the bikes, kickstands down, engines off.

Spc. Carl A Trice has completed his final journey.

Respectfully submitted,

David (Wild1) Shreckengost

Ride Captain

Patriot Guard Riders.

Two days later, the Patriot Guard Riders assembled to pay a final farewell to a fallen Hero.

Final Ride Report – Spc. Carl A. Trice, 4 June, 2014

It was a long day, but a very good day. This mission had a lot of moving parts, and some of them had to be improvised on the spot, but everything came together, and this was as smooth a mission as I have ever participated in.

While one group of Patriot Guard Riders was assembling at the Civic Center in Thomaston, Ga, putting out dozens of static flags, and preparing for the arrival of Spc. Trice's' family, another group was gathering 50 miles to the north, preparing to escort the family. All three of the other bikes were there when I rolled up 30 minutes ahead of the designated staging time. State Captain David Blanton, Asst State Captain for SE Ga, Don Wilson, and Ride Captain Robert Hammock had all gotten up early on a Sunday morning, left their families and loved ones behind, to ride to Hampton Ga, because a family needed to know that they were not alone in their grief. And so, they came.

The Henry County Police motor unit was a bit more prompt, they rolled up with four motorcycles just three minutes ahead of the designated staging time, and we were very glad to see them. When you are about to convoy a limousine and about 20 family cars across five different jurisdictions, you cannot have too many angels with blue lights, you just can't.

We got a few minutes to chat with these officers, all of whom had taken their own time to come and do this escort, then it's time to roll, and we fire up 8 bikes, almost in unison, and make the short drive to the family home. Then it's hugs, handshakes, "Thank you for coming", and you understand a little better why we do what we do. Then the Funeral Director calls everyone together at the foot of the driveway, and almost 60 people joined hands in prayer. That was a first for this Ride Captain, and it was a powerful moment.

"Amen, and Amen". And we're walking back to our bikes to head toward Thomaston, when I look up, to see the four Henry County Officers, who have just finished praying with the family, arms on each other's shoulders, huddled up on the sidewalk next to their motorcycles, praying. These are big, burly guys, the type you would not want to get into a fight with, huddled in prayer, it gave me a whole new respect for these men in blue.

And prayers were answered. We rolled out of Hampton on schedule, the Henry County officers smoothly handling traffic control duties. Got to the Spalding County line, a Spalding County Sheriff's Deputy is waiting, takes the lead. Spalding County has every intersection sealed off with a marked unit, till we hit the City of Griffin, then every intersection is sealed off with a City of Griffin Police unit, many of the officers standing at attention, and saluting as we passed by. Spaulding County stays with us all the way to the county line, where a Pike County Sheriff's Deputy is waiting to take the lead.

Thru Zebulon, where the Zebulon Police have the only major intersection sealed off, and down to the Upson County line, where there are not one, not two, but three Sheriff's Deputies, and a Ga State Patrol trooper awaiting us.

Down thru Thomaston, where the Thomaston Police Dept joined in, block intersections, and smoothing the way. Past the Courthouse, left turn, another, and then a right, and we're heading up the long driveway to the Civic Center. Flags greet us at the entrance, and flags line the side of the driveway as the motorcade comes to a halt, with the family limousine directly in front of the glass doors.

The remainder of the family assembles under the portico of the Civic Center, and slowly makes their way inside. The limo doors open, the Patriot Guard comes to attention and renders honors. The doors close, the music starts, the flag line fades away. Ride Captain Lee Love had everything set up and ready to go, and it was an impressive display,

Flags are rolled up, stowed away. All the static flags have to be gathered up as well, and all hands pitch in to get it done. Then, while most of us sit and wait, Bruce Tamker and his sidekick head down to the cemetery, to get set up for the graveside service to follow. More moving parts, it's just what we do.

Waiting. We do a lot of it in the Patriot Guard, and today was no exception. Give us time to tell stories, reflect on other missions, "you remember that time we –"and another story is being retold. Time seems to pass slowly under the sprawling oak tree, but finally the word comes, and we assemble once more in front of the Civic Center, only to find that the casket has been wheeled out the side door, despite what the Funeral Director had told us earlier.

Mount up, engines fire up, police sirens wail, and the short ride to the cemetery is underway. Around the square, past the Courthouse, again, down the hill on Hwy 19, right turn into the cemetery. Park the bikes on a convenient walkway, jump off, grab a flag, and get set up at the gravesite.

The Honor Guard, slowly and precisely, lifts its precious burden, and carries it to its final resting place as honors are rendered once again. A brief message from the 82nd Airborne chaplain, a prayer, then from on the hill behind us comes a voice like thunder: "SGT SMITH" from the group of soldiers assembled behind the hearse comes the answer, "HERE, 1ST SERGEANT", 'SGT WILLIAMS', "HERE, 1ST SERGEANT"

"SGT TRICE", no response, "SGT CARL TRICE", again, no response "SGT CARL A TRICE". Silence. Then, behind us, we hear rifles being loaded, and the air is split by the sound of gunfire. Again, and once more, "PRESENT ARMS".

The brief, haunting notes, of that familiar short anthem, "Taps" float across the assembled family and friends in an almost visible wave. Heads bow, eyes are dabbed, the finality of the moment has taken hold.

Rain had been predicted all day, and we had seen a few sprinkles, but as the Honor Guard lifted the flag from atop the casket, preparing to fold it, angel tears began to fall, but they seemed to fade away as the last folds were made, and the Sergeant-Major of the 82nd Airborne Division steps forward, drops to one knee, and says a few words to a grieving mother. A condolence book is presented to his mother, and another for his sister, a closing prayer, "Amen and amen", and the service is over.

Flags are rolled and stowed away, rebar for the static flags goes in its own case. Handshakes, hugs, "see you one the next one", "be careful going home", and the Patriot Guard rides away. Each one with their own memories of this day, a day when they could have been anywhere else, but they stepped forward and for one family, in Central Georgia, they made a difference, the depth of which they will never know, but God knows, and us, that's enough.

It was my honor to ride with them, to stand beside them, and to call them my brothers and sisters. I am humbled to be in their presence.

Respectfully submitted,
David (Wild1) Shreckengost
Ride Captain, Patriot Guard Riders

Burying a Law Enforcement Officer who has been killed in the line of duty is one of the toughest missions that the Patriot Guard Riders ever get asked to do, but one that we accept with honor and respect. It's the least we can do.

RIDE REPORT – SGT. CHRISTOPHER MONICA

E.O.W. 6/13/2017 SERVICES - 6/19-20/2017

Sometimes it seems like the simpler the Patriot Guard Mission is, the harder it is to write a ride report. This was probably one of the most straight forward missions that had come along in a while. As I told those who were at the mission briefing at the church on Tuesday, June 20, "there are not a lot of moving parts to this mission", and yet it was one of the most moving missions, and one that had a profound impact on everyone in attendance.

A bit of background information is in order here. When the news first broke about two officers from the Georgia Dept of Corrections being overwhelmed and murdered by two inmates that they were transporting, there was an immediate resonance. My beloved better half, known to most of the Patriot Guard as Mystic K, had spent most of her working life with the Georgia Dept of Corrections, where she was the Warden's secretary at Calhoun State Prison in Morgan, Ga, and it was there that she meet her late husband, who was in charge of training for the Corrections officers at that prison, up until he was forced to retire due to cancer, to which he later succumbed. Kay still wears a Dept of Corrections patch on her vest, along with his name tag, in honor of his service, and that is as it should be.

So when the tragic news broke, there was no doubt in my mind that we would have to participate in honoring these officers, should an invitation from the family be forthcoming, and when it was, I immediately volunteered to take the second of the two missions, and set about determining what needed to be done to properly honor Sgt. Christopher Monica.

As it turned out, "there weren't a whole lot of moving parts" to this mission. Basically, all we were asked to do was show up for visitation on Monday evening at the funeral home in Milledgeville, and then show up again for the funeral service, and graveside service at the First United Methodist Church, with burial taking place at the cemetery almost directly across the street.

Unfortunately, standing a flag line in honor of, and in recognition of the service of someone who has given ten years of his life to serving the people of the State of Georgia, is not glamorous, or exciting, and the result was a mere handful of Patriots felt sufficiently motivated to undertake the task, yet their presence was duly noted and appreciated by Sgt. Monica's family. His brother could not say enough good words about those dedicated souls who came and stood, and when his wife talked to me briefly as our flag line was winding down, she told me through tears how much it meant to her that we had come, and all the money in the world can't buy the feelings you walk away with under those circumstances.

The weather forecast on Tuesday morning, June 20, 2017 was 'rain, rain, and more rain', and your first thought as a Ride Captain is, 'great, nobody is going to show up, because nobody wants to ride in the rain'. Fortunately, this was not the case, as a goodly delegation of Patriot Guard Riders got in their four wheeled vehicles and made their way to Milledgeville, despite the rain, knowing it was the right thing to do.

We did have one brave soul who decided to throw a leg over, and rode his motorcycle all the way from Alabama to attend his very first Patriot Guard mission. Paul Harland has been a friend to our own 'Poppa Joe', and when he heard Poppa Joe was going to be in Milledgeville, he just had to come too, and it was our honor to welcome him into our somewhat dysfunctional family.

Mission briefing is held in front of a tent put up by the New Jersey State Police Benevolent Society, who brought a huge concession trailer all the way from New Jersey, and they served ice water, Gatorade, chips, cookies, and hot dogs to all who asked. No charge. I promised them I would never say anything bad about New Jersey ever again. And I meant it. Those folks were awesome. Rain had been light, and scattered up until this point, but as the briefing concludes, and the flags head down the hill to the church entrance, the bottom fell out, and it appeared as if it would continue like that for the remainder of the day.

The church lobby and entrance were packed with Corrections Officers and Police and Sheriff's deputies from across the country, all with one mission, to honor a fallen brother. South Dakota got the prize for furthest distance. Oklahoma, Massachusetts, Texas, Louisiana, Florida, Pennsylvania, Virginia, New Jersey, Michigan, and I am sure there were others. All with one purpose. The brotherhood in blue extends even behind the prison walls, and it was an inspiring sight.

The 'whoop, whoop' of police sirens tells us that the family is arriving, and the flag line come to attention, even as the rain continues to pour down. Doors open, big umbrellas pop out, and the family scrambles toward the entrance, as honors are rendered, by the Patriot Guard, and the assembled LEO's.

A steady procession of visitors, both uniformed and civilian continue to stream in under the ever-present umbrellas, and golf carts are ferrying folks who have had to park a considerable distance away. Finally, the first notes float out thru the open doors, and the service is underway, so the flag line quietly troops back up the hill. There are only a few moments to relax, and then we are walking down to the road, and across the street, setting up static flags to line the route that Sgt. Monica will take to his final resting place. Almost 50 static flags don't set themselves up, and all hands pitch in to get them in order, and despite the continual rain, the flags are a beautiful sight as they line the gravel drive.

We wait. Under a tree, rain still falling steadily, and the tree isn't much protection, but we do the best we can. It's not long until we get the word that the service is over, and the procession to the cemetery is underway. We grab our still wet flags and form our flag line between the static flags, and have barely taken our places before the sound of the bagpiper, who is leading the procession, falls on our ears. The music gets steadily louder, and then underneath it, you hear the soft clump of horse hooves, as the flag draped coffin is being carried on a horse drawn carriage.

The piper steps aside, the horse and carriage stop directly in front of us, the Dept of Corrections Honor Guard steps forward, and all come to attention and render honors, as they gently and carefully carry their fallen brother to his final resting place. The family is quietly seated, the pain on their faces visible for all to see. The minister has a few words, the familiar 'ashes to ashes, dust to dust', and then the Honor Guard steps forward again.

The flag is raised, held aloft, and the sound of rifles being racked, "FIRE", the sharp crack of seven guns, "Fire", and again. Then, that sound, those familiar, haunting, notes float out across the assembled crowd, and eyes get misted up, and something besides rain slides down the cheeks. The flag is folded, slowly, precisely, and the Officer in charge kneels in front of Sgt Monica's widow, and places that flag in her trembling hands. A condolence book is presented from the Patriot Guard Riders, along with a flag case that was made by the Middle Ga Woodworkers Association, specifically for the Patriot Guard to give to families in this circumstance.

A final prayer, and the service is over, and the crowd slowly disperses. The flag line slowly makes its way back to Poppa Joe's truck, and the very wet flags are rolled up and stowed away. Then we back track, pick up the static flags, pull the rebar, roll the flags up, and get them packed away as well.

Handshakes, hugs, many of the officer's present shaking our hands, telling us 'thank you', and us thanking them for what they do every day. A final 'see you later', 'see you at the next one', because we know there is going to be a next one. As long as America's finest stand for us, be they Military, Police, Fire, EMS or Dept of Corrections, the Patriot Guard will, if invited, stand for them.

It was an amazing group of Patriots who made their way to Milledgeville Georgia on a rainy Tuesday afternoon, and it was my privilege to stand beside them, and to call them my friends.

A tip of the Ride Captains hat to Willie 'Poppa Joe' Black, who drove up from Valdosta Ga to bring flags, as well as Dee Anderson, who came from Augusta Ga for the same reason. Roger, whose last name I did not get, brought eight cadets from the Ga Challenge Youth Institute to stand the flag line at the church, and they stood in the rain and got soaked like the rest of us. All who came and stood, rode away with the knowledge that they were where they were supposed to be, and for a few moments, for one grieving family, they had made a difference. Patriot Guard Riders – we do it because it's the right thing to do.

Respectfully submitted,
David (Wild1) Shreckengost
Ride Captain, Patriot Guard Riders

When another biker is killed, it has an effect on all of us who love to ride. Each and every one of us, deep inside, is thinking, "That could have been me". So, we come, and stand, with honor and respect, because it's the right thing to do.

Ride Report, Chris Stanfield, USMC, July 28/29, 2017

"Biker Down" are words that none of us want to hear, but on a Tuesday evening in Lamar County, Ga. The call went out, "Biker Down". This biker was William Christopher Gordon Stanfield, taken way too early in a tragic accident. Paramedics did all they could, they even life-flighted him to Grady, but "Chris", as he was known to his friends, will be forever 27.

Any time a mission request comes in, and it involves a biker going down, that always hits a little closer to home to those of us who enjoy the freedom of steels wheels, and when the request has the city you live in most of the week on it, you don't turn it down.

Visitation took place on Friday evening, July 28, 2017, and eleven dedicated Patriots laid aside their other duties and commitments to come to Jackson, Ga, and stand a flag line in Chris's honor. And an honor it was. A steady stream of visitors conveyed to everyone there that Chris was well regarded in the community, and the community turned out to support his family in their hour of grief.

Rain was forecast for Friday evening, but thankfully, none came until visitation and the obligatory meal following every Patriot Guard mission was complete. Then the bottom fell out, but it seemed to wash away a little of the hurt, and Saturday dawned a beautiful, unseasonably cool day for July in Georgia, and the promise of a new day was a welcome one for those Patriot Guard Riders who came from far and near, to a beautiful, huge church, which sits smack in the middle of nowhere.

Rock Springs Church will see approx. 2500 people pass thru its doors on a Sunday morning, and on this Saturday, it seemed as if almost that many bikes were going to show up. All thru the morning, they came, one, two, a small group, a large group, but they came, with one mission. Respect. A fellow biker had gone down, and the biker community rallied in his honor.

Combat Vets MC, Bomber Girls, Long Riders MC, and another group that had shirts specifically honoring Chris were among the almost 100 motorcycles that made their way to Milner, Ga to stand for a man that most had never met.

Static flags are placed along the sides of both entrances to the church, and there is just enough breeze blowing to make them stand out brilliantly in the bright morning sun. Just as the last flag was going up, the hearse came over the rise, and everyone came to attention and rendered honors as it turned in, made the left turn, and came to a stop under the portico. There were no pallbearers present, so the Patriot Guard Riders jumped in, and saw to it that Chris was safely transported into the church. And then it was time to unload the flower van, and a steady stream of leather clad bikers carrying flowers got the job down quickly, but it was a sight to behold.

Back outside, where the morning sun is making it warm enough that you want to go back into the church again. A short briefing, even as more bikes are making their appearance, and then the flag line sets up. Most riders are at the main entrance, but this church has four doors, and we had the people to cover all of them.

A roar of motorcycles lets us know that the family is approaching, and once again, all present come to attention and render honors as Chris's family arrives to say their final farewells. Again, a steady stream of people pour into the church, and many stop to say 'thank you', to those who are standing, flag in hand, expecting nothing in return, but knowing that there is no place that they would rather be. Time seems to pass so slowly, and the sun continues to shine even hotter, but at last the first notes begin to float out of the auditorium, and the flag line can stand down.

Flags are quickly rolled up and stowed away. Static flags and rebar disappear in a hurry, with this many people around, and in just a few minutes, Flag Wagon Man Bill Dowden is heading to the cemetery back on the other side of Jackson, to prepare for the graveside services to come.

Waiting. Maybe the hardest part of any mission, but we wait, swap stories, tell a few tall tales, and probably a few lies, but that's just how we roll.

Word comes that the service is over, and everyone gathers at the main entrance, and render honors once again, then it's, "Mount Up" and across the parking lot, the rumble and roar of engines sounds like music to the ears. The Funeral Director gives the signal, and Lamar County Sheriff's Deputies lead us up the hill, and Chris Stanfield is rolling out for the last time.

Riding thru the Ga countryside, you could almost forget the solemn occasion, until you glance in the mirror, and that long double line of headlights behind you, and your heart swells, knowing that all these bikes are here to honor a fallen brother. One we never met, but our 'two wheel' brother, just the same.

Left on Hwy 36, down the hill, where two Butts County Sheriff's cars pick up the escort. Roll thru Jackson, Jackson Police have every intersection covered, left turn, over the tracks, and back out into the beautiful farming country that is rural Ga, and that long line of headlights is still looking so awesome in the mirror.

Another left turn, a right into the cemetery, loop around and park on the road, even as bikes are continuing to stream into the cemetery. Up the hill, grab a flag, get everyone in position. The back door of the hearse opens, "PRESENT ARMS" brings everyone's hand up in salute. The pallbearers, led by one uniformed Air Force Sgt, and a uniformed Marine Sgt, struggle with the uneven terrain, as they carry their friend and brother to his final resting place.

The minister says a few words, trying to be as comforting as he can, but comfort seems to have taken absence, as the family seems almost inconsolable. Two Marines step forward, the flag is held aloft, and then those unmistakable, mournful notes, bring tears to those whose faces were unmarked to this point. The flag is folded, slow, precisely, and then the Sergeant turns, kneels before two small children, a boy, age 7, and a girl, age 5, lays the flag down so that it is touching both of them, and it was a good half minute before he could say a word. There was not a dry eye to be found anywhere in the vicinity.

He finally managed to get the words out, steps back and salutes and the tears were steadily flowing down his cheeks as he turned, and marched away. A Challenge Coin was presented to his mother, on behalf of our National President, Rob "Bees" Butler, who had helped escort the hearse, and was standing on the flag line a few yards away.

A few minutes more, and the service is done. The flag line slowly fades away; flags are rolled and stowed again. Again, the static flags and rebar are gathered up, put away. Hugs, handshakes, "see you next time", "careful going home", and the ever present, "Where we going to eat"? Because we are the Patriot Guard, and that's just how we roll.

No mission comes together by itself, and a tip of the hat to Daryl, "Big Dog" Gunter, who helped "Bees" with the hearse escort. Jeremy Shirah, John Hartman, and Ruben Hamilton, who escorted the family to the church, then Jeremy and John, did double duty escorting the hearse as well.

But the true "Thank You" goes to all those anonymous flag holders, whose names don't get mentioned in ride reports, but they come, they stand in silent honor, and they ride away, knowing in their hearts that they were where they were supposed to be, and for one family, mourning a son taken too soon, they made a difference, the scope of which none of us will truly ever know. It was my honor and privilege to stand beside them, and to ride with them, and for that, I am truly grateful.

They are the Patriot Guard Riders, and none of this is possible without them. THANK YOU.

Respectfully submitted

David Shreckengost, Ride Captain

Patriot Guard Riders.

For four decades teams of specialists have been searching some of the most inaccessible places on earth for the remains of missing American Servicemen. This organization, known as Joint POW/MIA Accounting Command, or JPAC has so far returned more than 1,800 missing servicemen and women to their families.

Ride Report – Sgt. Stafford L. Morris, MIA/POW Aug 12, 2017

It began, like most missions do, with a phone call, and it ended like most missions do, with the crack of rifle fire, and the haunting notes of that little melody called "Taps", and in between we got to pay our respects to a young man from Lehigh Pennsylvania, who wanted nothing more than to be a soldier.

Stafford Morris found himself in a cold, desolate place called Korea in Nov. of 1950. His unit, Battery A, 503rd Field Artillery, 2nd Division, United States Army, was north of Kujang-dong, Korea, when the Chinese Communist Army swarmed over the border, and the Americans were pushed back. As the unit retreated, they passed thru an area known as the 'gauntlet', and somewhere around Dec. 1, Sgt Morris was captured. He died in a prison camp on Jan 21, 1951 at the age of 24. He will always be a soldier.

Sixty-five years later, his remains were discovered in an unmarked grave, and identified thru DNA testing. Sixty-six years later, at the request of his remaining family, the Patriot Guard Riders assembled at a beautiful new church in SW Atlanta's Vine City neighborhood, to join his family in paying final respects to the young man they affectionately called 'lil bubba".

It was a beautiful late summer August Saturday, this lovely new church had just opened, it was built to replace one that was on the site of the new Mercedes Benz stadium, which is visible off to your left as you walk up to the main entrance. The gleaming skyscrapers of downtown Atlanta rise behind that, and it's a day when all seems right with the world.

Then a hearse rolls up, a flag draped casket is gently unloaded and wheeled into the church, as the Patriot Guard stands at attention and renders honors, and we remember why we are here, and the sacrifice that was made on our behalf.

A short briefing, the pledge, and a prayer, and the flag line takes its place at the entrance, with just enough breeze to help cut some of the summer heat, and enough shade to accommodate everyone. A smattering of mourners, the church ladies, all dressed in white, most of the others in black, trickle in, most seem somewhat surprised by the bikers with flags in this neighborhood. At almost 11 am, two limousines carrying the remaining family members of Sgt. Morris arrive, and they file slowly into the church, led by Sgt. Morris's older sister, supported by two nephews. The doors close, the music begins, the flag line fades slowly away.

Flags are rolled and stowed, static flags and rebar, likewise. "Get some more water before I leave" say's our flag wagon man, Bill Dowden, and we head his advice, before he leaves for the cemetery.

Then it waiting, and most are wise enough to assemble in the shade offered by the roof above the main entrance, and we swap stories, make phone calls, check your Facebook page, post an update, but mostly wait. And wait. And wait some more. It's not glamorous, it's not exciting, it's just what we do. We wait.

Finally, the Funeral Director gives us a thumbs up, and the waiting is over. Six Patriot Guard Riders line up at the door, and have the honor of carrying Sgt. Morris to the hearse, as others stand and render honors. The door closes, and the scramble is on. Get your helmet, gloves, secure your saddle bags, everything in place, the engine roars to life, and here we go.

Winding thru the narrow streets of Vine City, a lot of respect being shown as cars stop to let a Hero pass by. Down another street, around another corner, and out onto a main road. A couple more turns, the line of bikes and cars snakes its way across Atlanta, and it's one final left, and up the steep driveway of the cemetery.

Circle thru, and then a sharp left, as Mr. Bill has picked us out a prime parking spot. Off the bike, grab a flag and come to attention as the Army Honor Guard slowly and precisely executes the maneuver of carrying Sgt. Morris to his final resting place.

It's a brief service, and it ends like most do, "ready", "aim", "fire". Three times the commands are barked out, and three volleys are fired. Then the bugler lifts his instrument, and once again, those 24 haunting notes signify that another Hero has been laid to rest, this one was sixty-six years in the making.

It was my honor to be there, to stand alongside some of the finest Patriots I know, and to pay final respects to a young man who wanted nothing more than to be a soldier.

Respectfully submitted,
David (Wild1) Shreckengost
Ride Captain, Patriot Guard Riders

The weather once again managed to rear its ugly head, but the Patriot Guard Riders didn't let the weather interfere with them completing the mission, with honor and respect. It's just what we do.

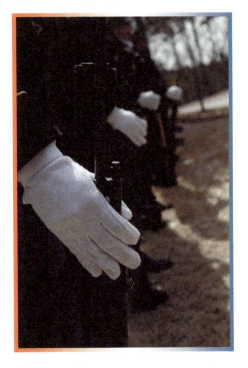

Ride Report – Cpl. Jesse Barber USA, 31 Aug, 2017

Patriot Guard missions sometimes seem to take on a life of their own, and this one was no exception. From the first email request for a Ride Captain, until the final presentation of a condolence book, and the handshakes at the cemetery, this one just seemed to be special.

Jesse Barber was a young man when he stepped forward, raised his right hand, and swore to protect and defend the United States, and he did so to the very best of his ability. After he left the Army, Jesse made a career out of body work on cars, and raised a family that knew what it meant to serve. Jesse's only son followed his Dad into the Army and made a 30-year career out of it. Both of his girls made successful careers for themselves, one in law enforcement, and the other in education, and they all attributed their success to the way that they were raised.

On a day when the weather forecast was for 80% rain, and more rain, 14 Patriots put aside what would have been their regular life, and made their way to the south side of Conyers Ga, at the request of Jesse's family, to honor his service, and let his family know that we stand alongside them in honoring a man, a father, a husband, a Soldier.

The mission itself was pretty straight-forward, only intermittent sprinkles greeted the Riders as they pulled into the parking lot. And while it wasn't raining heavily, it was one of those mornings that "you could cut the atmosphere with a knife" as my dad used to say.

On a more personal note, if you will allow. It was at this very Funeral Home, approx. 10 or 11 years ago, that I first encountered the Patriot Guard Riders. I was living at the time with (one of the ex-wives, I forget which one) in a subdivision and one of my neighbors was a man named Stan Shaw. Stan had a motorcycle (I was between motorcycles at the time) and was telling me about this group he had joined, and it went in one ear and out the other, as I was busy at this thing called 'life' at the time.

Long story short, Stan was killed when his motorcycle went out of control while he was on vacation, and when the ex and I went to the funeral home for the visitation, there were these 'biker' types standing outside holding flags. I found out then that these were the Patriot Guard Riders, and I told the ex (I think it was # 3) that when I got another motorcycle, I was going to join them and do cool stuff like that. Famous last words!

The 'cool' stuff got even cooler today. Fourteen Patriots, standing tall, with 'Old Glory' catching just enough breeze to make her show off her best, even in the misty morning rain. A small handful of family and friends pass thru the flag line, most seem surprised by our presence, but the words "thank you" are heard often. The arrival of two Rockdale County Sheriffs cars tells us that the limousines carrying the family have arrived. They park under the portico at the side of the Funeral Home, and march into the Chapel enmasse, as we rendered honors.

The doors close, the music starts, and the flag line stands down. Roll 'em up, put 'em away, and then we wait. Pat, Shaggy and John make a run to McDonalds, and a sausage egg biscuit and orange juice really hit the spot while we wait. And tell stories, and wait.

Rockdale County deputies told us before they left that they would be back at 11:45 for the escort to Ga. Veterans Memorial Cemetery, so we were expecting a lengthy funeral service, when suddenly, the side doors of the Chapel open, and even as we scramble to get into position, the flag-draped coffin emerges, and all come to attention, and render honors.

The hearse door closes, and we're scrambling for bikes at 11 am, knowing that the service in Milledgeville is scheduled for 2:30. It takes a while for the order of march to get lined up, and then the Sr. Funeral Director showed up, and decided to change the whole line up, so we're scrambling again. Semper Gumby, the motto of the Patriot Guard.

Finally, we're rolling out the drive, left turn on Hwy 138, and under the watchful eye of Rockdale's finest, and with our own Sid "Squirrel" Kelly, and David "Hi-Tech Redneck" Andrews running tail gunners, we rolled thru Conyers and onto I – 20 East with no major problems.

The 83-mile trip to the Georgia Veterans Memorial Cemetery was the longest two hours and fifteen minutes on a motorcycle in recent memory. Rain managed to hold off until just outside Eatonton on Hwy 441 south of Madison, the bottom fell out, and we were soaked to the skin when we arrived. (Note to self – rain suit in the saddlebag is not really effective)

So, here we are, one hour and forty-five minutes ahead of schedule, so we wait. Again. Fortunately, the rain has moved out, and it's a semi-pleasant afternoon, as we wait. There were no other services on the schedule, and apparently the family decided to go ahead with the service, so we set up a flag line again, and again rendered honors as the flag-draped casket rolled slowly into the Chapel at the cemetery, and the family slowly files in, knowing that this will be the last good-bye to a husband, father, grandfather, friend, beloved patriarch.

The minister has a few words to say, then the Honor Guard steps up, raises the flag, and as the rear doors of the Chapel open, the familiar haunting notes of "Taps" seem to reverberate from every beam in the ceiling of the vaulted Chapel. As the last notes fade away, the flag is snapped taut, turned, folded together, and then held flat, then slowly and precisely folded into a perfect triangle. The Sgt turns, kneels, "On behalf of the President of the United States, and the United States Army, please accept this flag in honor of your loved one's service to our country". He steps back, salutes, clicks his heels together, marches slowly away. A condolence book is presented, and the service is over.

Jesse Barber will rest forever beneath the pines east of Milledgeville, amongst the ranks of Heroes who have gone before.

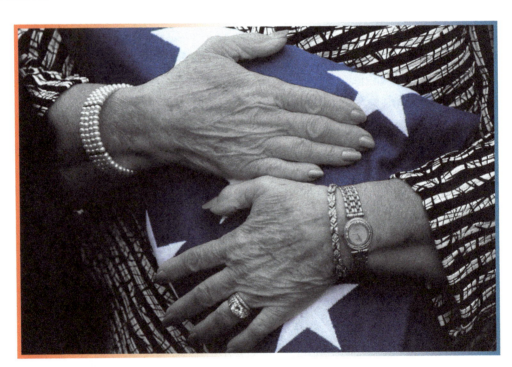

A tip of the Ride Captains hat to Pat White, who brought flags to Conyers, "Shaggy" Jay, John Hartman, Jimmy White, and Tony Cagle, who did an awesome 2 ¼ hr. four corners on the hearse, and the RC and the rest of the bikes got to see it from behind, thanks to Sr. changing the order of procession. To all who came, stood in the mist and rain, and rode off, I thank you. You are the Patriot Guard Riders, and none of this is possible without you. From the depths of my heart, "Thank You".

Sometimes, regardless of how much you plan, nothing goes as you want it to.

Enough said.

Sept. 24, 2017

Ride Report – 335th Signal Command

Every Ride Captain I know in the Patriot Guard Riders can tell you about that one mission that they've done, where everything went wrong, and it's no longer an exclusive club, as you will see. It began, as most missions do, the number flashes up on your phone, with the name of the Sgt from the 335th Signal Command Army Reserve Unit, out of East Point, Ga, and you know automatically, they have a group that's deploying, and they would like an escort to the airport.

Pick up the phone, and that's exactly right. No problem, date and time? Yup. Going to Atlanta Airport? Yup, Delta terminal? Yup, Same, same. We've done this at least seven or eight times, no problem. We'll be there. Pull up your notes from the last mission, okay, staging at the Citgo station, S. Main St, no problem.

A quick check of Goggle Maps reveals that it is now a BP Station. Opps, gotta change that. Okay, departure ceremony is at 10 am, we'll set staging for 9:30 am. Get it sent up to national for posting, Troop Departure Mission, Sept 24, East Point, Ga. good to go, right?

Friday, Sept 22, phone rings. 335th calling. Departure ceremony has been moved to 11 am, hope that's not a problem. No sir, no problem at all. Get on the computer, shoot a change of mission request up to National, get a response back that the Troop Welcome Home mission on Sept 25, in Augusta Ga, staging time has been updated to 10:30 am. OMG!!!

Send a reply back to National, point out their mistake, make phone calls to State Captain, and the RC involved in the Troop Welcome Home Mission, they in turn have to email National, and by Friday evening, we now have the correct staging time for two missions. Good to Go- right?

There was an empty chair on the left side, four rows back, at Gillionville Baptist on Sunday morning, but when you've got 68 American soldiers leaving their homes and families for one whole year, they needed to know that they had our support, the Lord will forgive us this time.

Arrived at the BP station, 15 mins ahead of staging, to find 10 scooters, and a Squirrel cage already in the parking lot. Did a short briefing, only one new rider, told him "this is quick and easy, we ride down, escort the bus to the airport, we go eat, nothing to it". Good to go – right?

Arrived at the Armory at the designated hour, 1100, normally, we have a reserved space right in front for motorcycles, nada. Not a parking spot to be had, no problem. Park the bikes right on the street. We're not going to be here long anyway. Good to go – right? At 1130 hrs., when we got an invitation to go inside for cake and punch, you began to get the feeling that this was not going down quite the way you thought it should. At 1145, which is the time that Atlanta Police were expecting us to roll up to the Delta terminal, we were told that the buses transporting the soldiers had not arrived yet. Busses roll in, 1155, okay, good to go – right?

Not so fast, "we've got a few more things to take care of". No problem. We wait. Waiting along with us were two of the East Point police's finest, and we learned a lot about the City of East Point. Finally, we have troops loading the busses, good to go – right? Nope! About this time a white heavy-duty panel van pulls up alongside the busses, and it's loaded with all their duffle bags, luggage, etc. etc. Okay, cool, they're going to follow the busses to the airport.

Wrong. At approx. 1215, everything on the panel van gets loaded into the cargo bays of the two busses, which was no easy task, these folks are going away for a year, they're taking a lot of 'stuff' with them. Finally, we've got the busses loaded with luggage and troops, motorcycle engines roar to life, a thumbs-up from the Sgt Major, and we're good to go – right?

Sort of. The East Point units, which have waited patiently with the rest of us, pull out, lights and sirens, the motorcycles fall in behind, left turn up the hill, ready to make the right turn, and the voice of one Sid " Squirrel" Kelly is coming over the CB radio, "The busses are not moving". Okay, so here we sit, two blocks from the Armory, no busses. After what felt like an eternity, finally the words we long to here, "the busses are rolling".

Okay, bike in gear, let out the clutch, turn right, left onto Main St, and our escort is finally under way. Easing down Main St, constantly checking the mirrors, sure enough, here come two busses. The East Point officers did an excellent job of getting us thru intersections, around the loop, down onto Lankford Pkwy, then I-85 south, hit Loop Rd exit, no problem. Airport terminal in sight, good to go – right?

Not exactly. Pull into the lower level, Delta terminal, Hartsfield Jackson International Airport, and there is no place to park. So, our East Point Officer hits the siren, and cars start to scatter like startled quail. It was a beautiful thing to see. He clears a space, we get the bikes stopped, wave the busses to the curb. Good to go. Wrong.

Another SgtMajor gets off the bus, "This is not where we're supposed to go". You've got to be kidding me. "No, we're supposed to be at 1200 Something or other St." Where the heck is that? East Point Police Officer Jordan to the rescue! "I know where that is", those words were music to my ears. "Can you lead us there", Sure, no problem.

Back on the bikes, slam helmet on, don't bother to fasten the chin strap, let's move. Out the end of the tunnel, back into airport traffic, and East Point is laying on the siren and moving people out of the way. Loop around the airport, to a small, private terminal, that I immediately recognized. The Patriot Guard had stood several flag lines here while receiving the remains of several fallen heroes, and it's a place that does not have happy memories for us.

We made some better memories today, as we parked the bikes, and walked to the busses. A female Warrant Officer, (and I apologize for not getting her name) asked to take a picture with all of us 'bikers', and of course, we couldn't say no. In the course of getting a bunch of unruly bikers gathered together, we learned that she had no family here to see her off, so we became her family for a few minutes. We all got hugs, and there were even a few tear stains, as we bid our soldiers farewell.

Thank God for men and women like these, who will step forward, raise their right hand and say, "Here am I, send me". If you feel the need to take a knee, do so with a prayer on your lips for the men and women of the 335th Signal Command. They are the true American Heroes, and it was our honor to send them off.

Respectfully submitted,
David (Wild1) Shreckengost
Ride Captain, Patriot Guard Riders

Honor Flight is one of the most enjoyable missions we get to do in the Patriot Guard Riders. We've meet so many interesting characters, that it would require hours to tell all their stories, but we know that they did what they did, for us, so that we could live in freedom. We owe them so much more than we can ever repay.

Honor Flight – Conyers: Ride Report 09/26/17

Honor Flight. How do you describe Honor Flight? If you are not familiar with them, the Honor Flight organization is a loosely knit group which operates all across the country, carrying primarily World War II veterans to Washington DC for a day, to view the monuments there and have a time of fellowship with other veterans. Because the World War II veterans are reaching the ages where it is difficult to find veterans who can physically make the trip, Honor Flight has been taking Korean War and some Vietnam veterans along with them.

There have been eighteen Honor Flights out of Conyers, and rumor is that this was going to be the last one, so this one was even more special.

This Honor Flight, # 18, was special, in a number of ways. From the earliest days of the Patriot Guard Riders in Georgia, Honor Flight missions were the sole propriety of our very own Ride Captain Larry (Laru) Klein, and he did a great job of organizing the Patriot Guard escorts, and seeing to it that the veterans got a great send off.

Because of the late hour that the veterans and their guardians arrive back in Atlanta, for the first couple years of Honor Flight, which was operating out of Fayetteville, Ga, that was all we did, was give them a big send off. Then Laru came up with the idea of meeting them at the airport and escorting them back to their original staging area, and the second part of this mission quickly became a favorite evening ride for many Patriot Guard Riders.

Due to some health issues, the Honor Flight missions managed to migrate to my desk, and when Laru was asked by the Honor Flight team to be a veteran on Honor Flight # 18, in honor of his many years of Honor Flight missions, you knew this one was going to be a little more special. Since Honor Flight began operating out of Conyers, the Rockdale County Sheriff's Dept has been an important part of getting the veterans and their guardians to the Atlanta Airport and back home again, and they commit a significant amount of resources, both in vehicles and manpower, to support the Honor Flight mission. When Sheriff Eric Levett showed up at the Conyers American Legion Post at 4 am on Tuesday, Sept. 26, in civilian clothes, and put on the red shirt that designated him as a guardian for one of the veterans going on the flight, it just made the mission even more special.

Another thing that made this one special is the man we all know as "Bugler". James Brannon, Patriot Guard Rider, United States Air Force Reserve, Firefighter/Paramedic – Clayton County Fire Dept, left home around 0200 hrs. to make Honor Flight Conyers, and he opened the ceremonies with 'Reveille' at approx. 0430, and somewhere around 2300 hrs., he closed the days ceremonies with a perfect rendition of that hauntingly familiar, "Taps", and veterans and guardians alike stood at attention. A most fitting ending to a very busy day.

Honor Flight begins gearing up somewhere around 0400 hrs., as veterans, guardians, staff, and the many officers from the Sheriff's Dept begin to filter into the American Legion Hall in Conyers. When the Sheriffs Dept trailer shows up, it's all hands-on deck, as we load the wheelchairs that will accompany each veteran, and make sure the count is correct. We have a story about waiting almost 20 minutes at the airport terminal while a stray wheelchair was rounded up, LOL.

We have stories, and we get to hear a few stories. Bill, a WW II veteran, said he enlisted at 17, because he knew he'd get drafted when he turned 18, and he didn't want to carry no rifle, so he joined the navy at 17. Jerry, who told the story of his recruiter turning down a blind recruit because his seeing eye dog had flat feet. Stories, more stories, one of the true joys of Honor Flight is getting to listen to the stories.

Our escort to Atlanta's Hartsfield – Jackson International terminal is about as uneventful a ride as one could expect, given the unforgiving nature of Atlanta drivers, and their seeming total disregard for a sea of blue lights provided by Rockdale County, but all 14 bikes, the bus, and the wheelchair trailer arrived without a scratch, and only a few choice colorful words being hurled at passing motorist.

Park the bikes, unload the wheelchairs, get your gate pass, and here we go. Take off your vest, take off your belt, take off your shoes, hopefully they won't ask you to take off anything else, or somebody might get embarrassed. Then you get to put it all on again, but thankfully, it's just a short stroll to the gate, where we get to hear more stories, shake some hands, get some hugs from our favorite Delta employees, and watch the sun rise thru the eastern windows.

All too soon, the boarding process begins, and the Patriot Guard lines up to shake hands some more, pat them on the back, and send them on their way. Then it's back thru the terminal, and believe me, bikers in the International terminal get a few looks from passers-by, back on the bike, roll down the hill, and over to the BBQ Kitchen for breakfast, because that's what we do.

The evening return escort rolls into the International Terminal as the last shreds of daylight fade over the horizon, and the control tower is awash in multi-colored lights. Bikes arrive, singly or in pairs, and then it's nothing to do but wait. Finally, a text from our favorite paramedic, "We are on the ground". Even then, it's a good 20 minutes before the first blue and red shirts appear, and this particular veteran told us, "I need a smoke". We figure he must have sprinted off the plane, because it was another 10 minutes before anyone else showed up.

Down the corridor they come, blue shirts, red shirts, everyone smiling, some walking, some enjoying the ride in the wheelchair, all of them buzzing about what a wonderful day it was. Round up the wheelchairs, load 'em in the trailer. Make sure the count is correct. Okay, we got 'em all. Everyone's on the bus, fire up the bikes, cue the blue lights, and here we go, with Rockdale County clearing the path for us once again.

Another uneventful ride back to Conyers, with the Rockdale County Fire Dept sitting on each bridge we cross under, lights on, men and women at attention, letting our veterans know that their service is appreciated. Up the exit ramp, left turn, every intersection sealed off, left, right, left, and we pull into the Legion parking lot, under a huge, brightly lit American flag, that is hanging from the snorkel truck, an almost breath-takingly beautiful sight, and there wasn't a soul anywhere taking a knee.

Park the bikes, unload the wheelchairs, make sure the count is right. A few closing words, and then "Bugler" does what he does so well, and what may be the last Honor Flight Conyers is in the books. Handshakes, "good job", and a special thank you the all the men and women from Rockdale County Sheriff, and Fire, for their excellent work, and it's off to IHOP, because, we are the Patriot Guard, and this is what we do.

Patriot Guard Riders, they don't do it for money, or fame. They do it because it's the right thing to do. They came from near and far, with one purpose, to honor those who have sacrificed so much for us. They are some of the best people you will ever meet, and they make all this possible. It was my honor to ride beside them, to break bread with them, the share this mission with them. I salute each and every one of them. They are my heroes.

Respectfully submitted,
David (Wild1) Shreckengost
Ride Captain, Patriot Guard Riders

Facebook has become an important tool in getting mission information out to some of our members, but in this case, Facebook was the starting point for this mission.

Ride Report, John Robert Lindsey, USCG, 16 Oct. 2017

When a friend's request pops up on Facebook, little did we realize that it would lead us to a small cemetery in Milner Ga, on a beautiful fall day that was made for riding motorcycles. Having no idea who Philip Lindsey was, the fingers went to the 'delete' button until the words, "Friend of Dennis Scott" popped up. Any friend of Dennis Scott is a friend of mine. Dennis Scott is one of the finest Americans I know, proud to call him friend.

Philip called to say that his grand-father had just passed away, and he would like the Patriot Guard to come and stand for him. John Robert Lindsey had enlisted in the United States Coast Guard with the expectation, as Philip told me, of chasing girls around the Caribbean, instead the young man from middle Georgia found himself in Anchorage, Alaska. Nevertheless, he put in four years active duty and two more in the reserves before coming home, settling down and raising a family.

Rain. It's a sound you don't want to hear at 5 am on the day when you've got a mission to go to, and you want to ride the bike, but that's exactly what we heard. The rain of 5 am had given way to intermittent sunshine when it came time to saddle up and head toward Griffin Ga, although the temperature hadn't yet matched the look of the weather, so a jacket was still required for comfortable riding.

Pulled into the Funeral Home parking lot, and there are already 3 bikes that we recognize, and a couple that we don't. Becky and Laru Klein are there with the flags, and the sun is starting to show itself a little more, and the day is looking better and better.

Bikes and cages continue to roll in, and when you've got fifteen flag-holders lined up along the walkway on a Monday, with very short notice, you can only stop and admire the dedication of these amazing people we call the Patriot Guard Riders. They all had other things they could have been doing, maybe should have been doing, but they laid it all aside, because the young kid in the white uniform, with the big smile on his face, the kid who thought he was going to be chasing girls around the Caribbean, the kid who served his country those many years ago, that kid was taking his final journey, and the Patriot Guard Riders, and the Southside Riders, were going to be there, to pay their final respects, and in their own way, say "Thank you" to the kid from Griffin who went off to Alaska because his country asked him too.

Visitation passes quickly, as the flag-line stands erect, just enough of the morning breeze left to make the flags stand out in the ever-increasing sunlight. We stand down as the service starts, and swap stories. We remember a hot day about three years ago when we stood under the portico of this funeral home and petted the horses that would soon carry a Griffin Police officer to his final resting place. It was a day that many of those present on this autumn afternoon will remember for the rest of their lives.

A 'heads up' from the funeral director, and the Guard falls in alongside the hearse, as our hero is carried out into the now brilliant sunshine. All come to attention and render honors, the casket slowly disappears, the door slams, and it's time to ride. Two cars from the Spalding County Sheriff's Dept are already lined up to go, and then another appears, and then another, but you can never have too many LEO's on an escort and they guided us thru Griffin without a hitch.

Right turn on 16, down the hill, out of town, over the tracks, and out into the countryside, flags flying, everyone in line, a beautiful, dignified procession snakes its way down to the cemetery next to Rock Springs Church. Becky and Laru are already there, and have the flags staged out in the hedges adjacent to the cemetery, so all we have to do is grab one and fall in on either side of the grave.

The minister says a few words, his closing prayer is longer than his closing remarks, but it's a heartfelt appeal to the Throne, and there are few dry eyes when he finishes. Two funeral directors step forward, raise the flag and fold it, slowly, carefully. You can tell they've done this before. One of them kneels, presents the flag to the daughter, and it's over. The kid from Ga in the white uniform, with the big smile on his face, is now at rest.

It was truly an honor to be invited to stand, ride, and in some small way, let a grieving family know that they are not alone in their sorrow, we sorrow with them, and we are grateful that men like John Robert Lindsey stepped forward, raised their right hand, and served their country. We truly owe them a debt that

we can never pay.

To the men and women of the Patriot Guard Riders, a hearty "Thank You". You make all of this possible, and for that I am in your debt.

Respectfully submitted,
David (Wild1) Shreckengost
Ride Captain, Patriot Guard Riders

One of the realities we run into in the Patriot Guard Riders is the fact that we sometimes have very limited numbers, due to a myriad of missions taking place at the same time, but we always say, "However many show up, it's always the right number".

Ride Report – Christopher Woodbury – 11/11/17

It was Veterans Day, and a Korean War Veteran was being laid to rest. It was a cloudy, overcast day, and the weather seemed to match the mood, as friends and family gathered at a small white concrete block church, in a small South Georgia town.

The Patriot Guard Riders had been invited to stand in honor of Sgt. Woodbury's service, but it was Veterans Day, with a myriad of activities going on to honor veterans, and many chose to be in other places, so two Patriot Guard Riders and one first-timer made their way to this little church, in this little town and paid final respects to a soldier who had stood for us many years ago in a far-away place called Korea.

He served his country well, Sgt. Woodbury did, earning a Bronze Star for valor in combat, before returning to his little town in South Georgia, to live out the rest of his life with his wife of 62 years, raising a family, and leaving a legacy of service to his country, that we could all learn from.

The little white church sits just off the paved road, from where we stood next to the front door, three steps would have put you in danger of being run over. The hearse is already parked, half on the street, half in the parking lot, as we roll up.

A smattering of static flags has already been placed alongside the street, and the wind is briskly blowing them straight out, with enough of a chill that you wish you had some gloves on.

A steady procession of cars arrives, and mourners' stream into the church, under the direction of the Funeral Home staff, who seem to be everywhere at once. "Thank you" is heard often, as the mourners recognize the flag holders, even tho they were few in number.

A siren alerts us to the arrival of the family, and as the limousine comes to a stop in front of the church, the Funeral Director is barking out orders, getting everyone in line, and the family enters the church in-mass.

The flag line fades away as the service begins. Flags are rolled, rebar pulled up, and the Ride Captain leaves State Captain David (Hound) Blanton and the newbie, Michael Paulk, to provide escort duties, as he proceeds to attempt to locate the City Cemetery. Thankfully, Google knows all, and he arrives with

more than enough time to place static flags around the gravesite, in this small, isolated cemetery. Eight flags, each one standing straight out in the brisk afternoon winds, add a small bit of badly need color to this otherwise bleak landscape.

Then there is nothing to do but wait. And chat with the Army Honor Guard, who has driven up from Ft. Stewart, because, apparently, all the National Guard Honor units got Veterans Day off, according to the Ft. Stewart fellows.

We swap stories, talk about where we call 'home', Michigan for the Sgt, the Spec is from Puerto Rico, the Private is from Alabama. Yet, like us, they're here for one reason, honor, earned on the field of battle, in a faraway place called Korea.

In the distance, finally, the 'rumble' reaches our ears, and we know the procession is drawing close. Over the hill, led by the blue lights of the Nicholls City Police, and the familiar rumbling of motorcycle engines, even tho there were only two.

The hearse come to a stop, and even as the flag line was getting into place, the flag draped casket is being carried to its final resting place, so we quickly snap to attention and render honors.

The Funeral Director is again barking out orders, getting the family and friends gathered around, I wonder if she used to be in the Army. A nod to the Ministers (I think there were 5, altogether) and they each have their own reading from the little book that they carried. A prayer from the last one, and the Military steps forward, the flag is raised, and very quickly folded, almost as if they were in a hurry to get done. The flag is presented to his daughter, the Sgt. Salutes, and walks away.

The Funeral Director announces that the service is over, and the ministers and pallbearers step around to comfort, and shake hands with the family. As the last pallbearer steps aside, the bugler lifts his horn, and those familiar mournful notes float out across the barren South Georgia landscape, and Sgt. Woodbury is laid to rest.

Veterans Day, 2017, will forever be, a small, wind-swept cemetery in South Georgia. The Patriot Guard Riders, tho few in number, came, stood, and honored a Hero from another time, a reminder that freedom is not free, and on this Veterans Day, there was no place they would rather be.

Respectfully submitted,
David (Wild1) Shreckengost
Ride Captain, Patriot Guard Riders

It was a busy year, but time spent honoring those who have "stood for us" is never time wasted.

CHAPTER ELEVEN — 2018

THIS ONE HIT REALLY CLOSE TO HOME

This mission in Jackson, Ga., was, literally, minutes away from my second home, as I am probably in Jackson more than I am at the SW Ga hideout. So, yes, this one was 'close to home'.

Ride Report – Carl M. Finney, Jan. 18, 2018

When the name "Don Wilson "flashes up on your caller id, you know this call is not about the weather, or how well did the University of Georgia do in basketball last night. Don is the SE Ga Assistant State Captain, and he has a request for the Patriot Guard to stand for a veteran, in Jackson, which is my second home, wants to know if I can take it.

Middle of the week missions are some of the hardest to do, because of the little thing called a J-O-B, but fortunately, things at the hospital are not quite so hectic, meaning that time off can be obtained, and then he said the magic words that sealed the deal, "He was a friend of Jerry Rape". That was all he had to say, Jerry has been a dedicated Patriot Guard Rider for many years, and serves as one of our Mentors for new people coming in, and any friend of Jerry is a friend of mine, and mission planning was on.

Weather is not usually the first thing on your mind when a mission request comes in, but it wound it playing havoc with this mission, as it arrived just in time to mess up most of the Atlanta area, and kept folks from coming out that might otherwise have been available.

The original mission plan was to have a flag line during visitation on Wednesday evening, Jan. 17, and since we knew far enough in advance that it was going to be quite cold that evening, we had advised the

Funeral Home that we would be standing inside, which was fine with them. What we didn't realize at the time was that winter precipitation was going to accompany the cold weather, and make driving, particularly on side roads, extremely tricky. After talking with Don Wilson, and reviewing weather and traffic reports, a STAND DOWN order was issued for the visitation portion of the mission.

"Stand Down" is not something we like to do as Patriot Guard Riders. We like to think of ourselves as a pretty dedicated and determined bunch of folks, but safety is also one of our top priorities, and with travel conditions being what they were, safety for our members had to take precedence, and we reluctantly stood down.

Fortunately, by midday on Thursday, Jan. 18, temps had climbed above freezing for the first time in two days, the sun was making travel more inviting, and a small but dedicated group of Patriots made their way to the Funeral Home in Jackson to honor a man who had stepped forward, and served his country to the best of his ability.

Wind chill factors were still pretty chilly as we set out static flags in front of the funeral home, but the wind and the sun made those flags really stand out as a steady stream of mourners arrived to say their last goodbye's to a man whom the Funeral Director told me, "was one of the best men I've ever known".

Six Patriots manned the front and rear doors to the Funeral Home, as everyone that passed thru the flag line and the words 'thank you' were heard repeatedly. An hour passed slowly in the very chilly Georgia afternoon, but finally we saw everyone inside heading to the chapel, and that was our cue that the first portion of today's mission was over, and we gratefully gathered up flags, and moved down the street to the cemetery, where the afternoon sun was doing its best to make it feel more like Georgia and less like Minnesota.
Waiting. We do a lot of it, and today was no exception. Once we had put out some static flags around the gravesite at the City of Jackson cemetery, there was nothing else to do but wait. We swap stories, and speculate about how long the service will last. We talk about the one where there were six preachers lined up to speak, so everyone knew that service was going to last awhile.

Jerry Rape and his wife Vicky had stayed at the Funeral Home for the service, since they had known Carl and his wife Barbara from church, so when we saw them pull into the cemetery we knew the procession would not be far behind, and the wail of a siren from a Butts County Sheriff's Deputy's car got everyone scrambling into position. The procession winds slowly thru the gate, and the hearse stops in front of the tent. Carl is carried to his final resting place as the mourners assemble under two blue tents.

Military honors were rendered at the Funeral Home, so the service at the graveside is relatively brief. The minister reads some scripture, speaks for just a few minutes, another minister addresses the family for a few minutes, then has a prayer, a condolence book is presented to Carl's wife, Barbara, on behalf of the Patriot Guard, and as a bagpiper plays "Amazing Grace", the service is over.

Flags are gathered and rolled up, stowed away. Handshakes, hugs, "See you next time", "be careful going home", because there will be a next time, and when invited, the Patriot Guard Riders will be there to stand again, because this is what we do.

A tip of the Ride Captain's hat to Jerry and Vicky Rape, Ride Captain Lee Love, Ferrell Jackson and his neighbor and riding buddy, Margaret, who took the time to come to Jackson Ga on a very cold Thursday afternoon to honor a man who had served his country. You exemplify the qualities of service that make the Patriot Guard such a special organization, and I salute each and every one of you.

Respectfully submitted,
David (Wild1) Shreckengost
Ride Captain, Patriot Guard Riders

Once again, we barely had time for the motor to cool off, before we're off on another mission, and this one also, was 'close to home'.

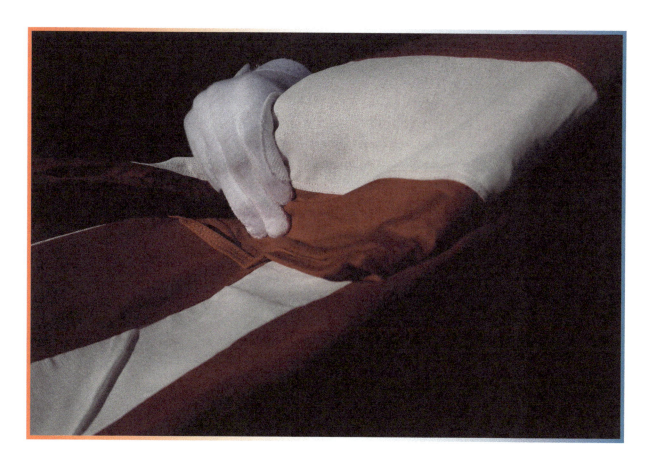

Ride Report – Home Dedication – Jan. 20, 2018

When the phone rings, you never know who or what is on the other end, but when the caller identifies himself as Commander Alton Head from American Legion Post 516 in McDonough, you sit up and take notice, and when the Commander says he would like for you to ride with him, you don't say no, just "what time, and where". And so, another Patriot Guard mission begins.

As a Ride Captain, you really have to appreciate those missions where someone else does all the heavy lifting, and all you have to do is show up. Commander Head had everything lined up, except for flags, and flags is something the Patriot Guard Riders do very well, so what he wanted to know was, "can you bring bikes with flags"? Oh, yes, we can. And on a Saturday morning that started off like Alaska and ended up like Florida, the Patriot Guard Riders brought bikes, and flags, and more flags.

This mission had actually begun back in May, when American Legion Post 516 was asked if they could help out with fixing the home of a Vietnam veteran in Barnesville, who was sleeping in his car during cold weather, because his house was in such poor shape. Even though Post 516 is in Henry County, and Barnesville is in Lamar County, the men of 516 exhibited the true character of veterans, in that they never leave a comrade behind, and they immediately went to work, to see what they could do to help their brother.

Four thousand + volunteer hours and approx. $32,000 later, Vietnam veteran John Greene has a home that is beautiful, inside and out. It is truly an outstanding example of what can be done when people won't take no for an answer, and the men and women of American Legion Post 516 truly exemplify that spirit, and it was our honor to stand alongside them, as they cut the ribbon on this house, and handed John Greene the keys to a beautifully remodeled home.

As stated earlier, Commander Head had done most of the work on this mission, so we literally didn't have to do anything but show up and ride. The thermometer was below freezing when most riders hit the road on a cold Saturday morning, but the sun shine was already giving us the promise of warmer temperatures, so a little morning cold was easier to tolerate.

Almost a dozen bikes were in the Food Depot parking lot upon our arrival, and more continued to arrive, until almost thirty bikes were lined up behind four Henry County Police Motor units, and flags were flying behind most of the bikes in line. After a brief safety briefing, the Pledge of Allegiance and a prayer from the Post Chaplain, it was time to roll. V-twin motors rumbled and roared, a 'whoop – whoop' from a police siren, and the procession was under way.

The Henry County Police Motor Unit is a well-trained group, and getting to watch them operate in traffic, and the way they smoothly hand their bikes, it is truly beautiful to see. I've been blessed to have a front row seat for several performances by them, and they are excellent at what they do.

We roll smoothly down Hwy 42, right turn at Bill Gardner Pkwy, thru morning traffic, and left turn onto I-75 South, roll south for a few miles to Hwy 36, with no problems. Off the ramp, Exit 201, right turn, down the hill, and rolling toward Barnesville, with Henry County Units seamlessly covering every intersection and possible hazard, and we rolled effortlessly up the hill, past the Barnesville City Limit sign, a final right turn onto Eleventh St, and we've arrived, along with about half of the population of Barnesville, it seems.

It takes a few minutes to wind the bikes through the congestion, and get everyone parked. Fortunately, we have arrived early, and we have some time to walk thru the house, view the before and after pictures, and truly appreciate the excellent job that Post 516 did.

Finally, the Master of Ceremonies ask everyone to take their places, and the Patriot Guard lines up with their flags, (provided by our own Bruce and Celia Tamker) along the walkway. There were a lot of people who contributed in one way or another to the success of this project, and I think the MC made sure that each and every one of them got mentioned. What had been originally thought to be a 15-20-minute ceremony, stretched out to over an hour, but looking at the expression on John Greene's face as he stepped up to help cut the ribbon on this 'new' home made it all worthwhile.

Ceremony over, we roll up and stow the flags, and then it's time, "let's eat". It's what we do best, and there is no finer group of people to break bread with then those who ride with the Patriot Guard. So off we go, carrying the smiling face of John Greene with us, and thankful for the invitation from Commander Alton Head to be there, and have a small part in letting one veteran know that there are other veterans who care about him, and will do whatever needs to be done, so that "no comrade is left behind".

Respectfully submitted

David (Wild1) Shreckengost

Ride Captain

Patriot Guard Riders.

Any time you have to ride up to Delta Cargo at Atlanta's Hartsfield-Jackson International Airport, you know it's not going to be fun and games. This was one of the most memorable escorts we have ever done.

RIDE REPORT – Pfc Ashton Fuller, 3/16/18

When you are sitting across the table at lunch after church with Epic Eric Bishop, and he says something like, "I might need your help with something" you don't expect that it is going to result in a most memorable Patriot Guard mission, but that's exactly what happened.

Epic laid out the details, 21-year-old Army Pfc, just married, sent to Korea, and now coming home for the last time. Heartbreaking, even hearing the story third-hand. Details are not important, Ashton Fuller stepped forward, raised his right hand, took an oath, and carried out his duties to the very best of his ability. He stood for us in a far-away place so we could sleep in peace, and the Patriot Guard Riders would be there to honor his service, and to let his family know that we honored and appreciated his service.

There was plenty of time to put this mission together, and Epic did most of the heavy lifting, but when the flight schedule kept getting changed, I sometimes questioned whether or not we would be able to mount an escort back to Ashton's home town of Manchester, Ga. But the Patriot Guard Riders are a hardy lot, and when staging time at the Atlanta airport was posted as being 12 Midnight, we had a few drop-outs, but most of those who had already committed to be there when staging was scheduled for 6 pm on March 15, still said "I'll be there", and they meant it.

The rumble of two-cylinder steel beast is heard over the roar of jet engines, as Patriot Guard Riders, Southside Riders, and others make their way down Maynard Jackson Pkwy, and pull up in front of the austere concrete structure that comprises Delta Air Cargo. It was a warm March day in Georgia, but the sun is long gone, and a chill is definitely in the air, as, motors roll in. They should all be at home in bed at this hour, but they are here, instead, for one reason Respect.

Each and every airport arrival we do is special, not just for the family that is receiving a fallen service member, but for those who ride in their honor, and this one was no exception. When the family procession arrived at Delta Cargo, accompanied by two Meriwether County Sheriff's deputies, and two City of Manchester Police units, we realize that this was a young man who made an impact, as the parking lot in virtually full of vehicles.

The US Army Honor Guard is already on-site, and they take up their positions just inside the cargo door labeled '60', even as the hearse is backing up the ramp. The family climbs the ramp and assembles in front of the cargo area. One of the advantages of this late hour is that there are no other vehicles moving in the area, so they have the place all to themselves.

The Delta Honor Guard has been on standby since 6 pm, and they, like the rest of us, should be at home in bed, but they're here, just as we are. Respect. We have almost an hour to wait, but finally there is word that the plane is on the ground. The immediate family moves inside the hanger, the rest gather at the open door, '59' the Delta Honor Guard has gone to bring Ashton off the plane, the rest of us, wait. The chill in the air seems to be getting a little colder. We wait.

Minutes seem like hours at a time like this, but finally, the flags of the Delta Honor Guard come into view, and directly behind them, the flag-draped coffin that we all wish wasn't really there. The family gathers around it for a few minutes, hugs, tears, touching the flag, not wanting to believe what their eyes are seeing, then slowly, they walk away.

The US Army Honor Guard steps forward with quick, precise steps, "halt", "face", and they slowly and carefully carry this young man, son, nephew, cousin, husband, to the waiting hearse as all come to attention and render honors.

The door closes, salutes are dropped, flags are carried back to the flag wagon, and then it's pull on the jackets, strap up the helmets, pull on the thickest gloves you've got, and fire up the motor, it's time to take this hero home.

At 1:23 am, blue lights lead the procession down the Parkway, left turn onto Loop Rd, and circle the airport to hit I-85 south. The lateness, or earliness of the hour works to our advantage, as Atlanta traffic, known to be some of the worst, is almost non-existent, and the Sheriff's Dept does an excellent job of managing a long string of vehicles, which is never an easy task under the best of circumstances.

"Listen my children and you shall hear, of the Midnight Mission to Manchester". And the old Greg Allman song about the "Midnight Rider" came into my head as we rolled steadily south, exit 41, left turn, Hwy 27 south, Manchester here we come. LEO's from a number of different agencies blocked intersections all along the route, and gave us smooth ride, thru towns small, and smaller, until a final series of turns put us in front of Cox Funeral Home, and Ashton Fuller was once again back in his home town. It is 3:03 am.

A tip of the Ride Captains hat to Epic Eric, who is the Ride Captain for this mission, Bill Dowden, the flag-wagon man that I can always count on, Shaggy Jay and John for directing traffic as we departed. Dennis Scott gets credit for the "Midnight mission to Manchester". Jim Seymour Allen Watson, Jerry Jameson ran tail gunner, it truly is a team effort and I thank each and every one of them.

But the biggest thanks go to those whose names don't make the ride report. They show up, they stand, hold a flag, and sometimes hold a crying relative, they mount up and ride, and then go to their homes, seeking no applause or congratulations, they are the Patriot Guard Riders, and none of this gets done without them. They are truly the unsung heroes; I salute each and every one of them.

Respectfully submitted,

David (Wild1) Shreckengost

Ride Captain

Patriot Guard Riders

Ride Report – Christopher Ray McGlauchlen 3/23/18

It begins, as most missions do, with a phone call, but this phone call was different in several ways. March 17, 2018 was a beautiful spring day in Georgia, a warm and breezy afternoon as MysticK and I were sitting on the back porch of the SW Ga hideout. For many people, whether they are of Irish descent or not, March 17 is a day of partying and revelry, but for the woman I love, it was not a happy day. Three months prior, on 17 December, she received the phone call that no mother should ever receive, and a frantic trip to the hospital in Sylvester brought her to a cold, sterile room where the body of her middle son lay, gone from here to the arms of his Heavenly Father. Jed Lee Kimbrel will forever be 36 years old.

So when the phone rang on 17 March, and the person on the other end of the phone was Dolores Berry Thrash, who is one of the Paramedics that accompany every Honor Flight Conyers as they take Veterans to Washington, DC, the tone of her voice immediately told you this was not your ordinary phone call. Another young man, a Marine Veteran, a Volunteer Fire Fighter, a Husband, Father, Brother, Son, had answered his last call, and had gone to his Fathers home above, and the family wanted the Patriot Guard Riders to be there to honor him at his funeral service.

Standing a Flag Line for a Visitation at a Funeral Home is not something we do because it's fun. It's not fun, it's not glamorous, but having so recently experienced being on the 'other side' of this, you know that just your presence means a lot to this grieving family. So, on a Friday night, when there is a myriad of other things that they could have been doing, six patriots made their way to a small Funeral Home on the outskirts of Madison, GA. Two hours pass pretty slowly when there is nothing to do but stand in one spot, but you got the sense of how many people Christopher had touched, as the parking lot was nearly full even before visitation officially started, and the constant stream of vehicles in and out, and the line stretching thru the chapel and out into the parking lot told you volumes about this young man.

Saturday, March 24, 2018, the Patriot Guard assembles again, this time in front of a white Baptist Church in rural Morgan County. The morning clouds have begun to give way to sunnier skies as they roll in, one or two at a time. Flag wagon man Bill Dowden has marked the entrance to the church and lined one side of the drive with American Flags, and they are a beautiful sight. Already parked in front of the church is an absolutely gorgeous tiny replica fire engine, built by the Morgan County Firefighters, on an extended golf cart frame. It is a beautiful piece of work that was obviously done with a great deal of care, and we learn from the Funeral Director that the casket will be carried to the gravesite directly behind the church on this small fire engine.

A quick briefing, the pledge, and a prayer, and the Flag Line assembles at the foot of the steep steps leading up to the church. Just as with the visitation the prior evening, folks are arriving early, and in numbers, another testament to the impact that this young man had on his community. It isn't long until a rumbling noise off to our right tells us that the procession carrying Christopher's' body from the funeral home is getting closer. The Funeral Directors car is first to make the turn into the church driveway, followed by four beautiful motorcycles, in perfect formation, flags flying in the morning sun, our hero arrives with honor.

The truck carrying the casket backs up to the steps as all come to attention. The Funeral Director gets the pallbearers lined up, each one getting a red rose pinned on his lapel. The trucks wooden gate is lifted away, a wooden gate made for this truck, for this occasion, by Chris' Uncle, and the flag-draped coffin is slowly and carefully carried up the steps, into the church as honors are rendered.

The family assembles at the base of the steps, and as they start up to enter the church, Chris' son sees Chris' mom, and yells out, "ya-ya, ya-ya". Kays grandson, James, calls her 'ya-ya', and when Landon yelled out to his grandmother, a 60+ year old Ride Captain lost it right there at the foot of the stairs, and the tears would not stop. People pour into the church until the Funeral Director comes to the top of the stairs and announces to those remaining that there is no seating left in the church, and those wishing to view the service can go to the Fellowship Hall where the service will be on video screens.

As the music starts, the Flag Line slowly fades away, flags are stacked beside the van, and ready at a moment's notice, then we do what we do a lot of. We wait. Some last-minute details are hammered out with the Funeral Director, some assignments are designated, we swap stories, we take a few pictures, and we wait. And wait.

Finally, a thumbs up from the Funeral Director, and the Flag Line reassembles at the base of the steps, alongside the remarkable replica fire truck, and all render honor as the casket is gently lifted into place. The little engine kicks over, and starts to move, and the Flag Line moves with it, flags flying into the breeze as a brisk pace is required to keep up. The little engine rounds the tent, the Flag Line splits off on either side, and the family slowly passes between and takes their places under the tent, immediate family has chairs, all others gather around.

One minister, a family relative from Idaho, steps forward and speaks for a few minutes, reminding all present of the brevity of life, and the assurance of Heaven for those who are Believers. Then the Marines step forward, dress blues looking sharp, the flag is held aloft, and once again, those twenty-four notes that still brings tears to our eyes, no matter how many times we have heard them before, they still stir something inside you, and you know that another Hero has taken his place in the eternal ranks, and a tear slides slowly down.

The flag is folded, slowly, precisely, as it has been done many times before. The First Sargent kneels, places the flag in the lap of a grieving widow, says a few words, stands up, salutes, and marches away. As he clears the tent, the radios carried by the Morgan County Firefighters, who are directly behind the now plain wooden casket, crackle to life, as the Dispatcher issues a 'last call'. It was a most unusual set of signals, and at one point, the Funeral Director thought that it was over, and motioned for the Patriot Guard to step forward so as to bring the service to a conclusion, when the Dispatcher came back on the radio, and finally delivered one of the best 'last call' broadcasts that I have ever heard, and it definitely had an impact on all who were present.

In quick succession, a teddy bear with a 'Mission Complete' pin was presented to Landon by "Hollywood, a book of condolences, a PGR Challenge Coin, and a Marine Corps pin were presented to his widow. "Bendusty" presented a PGR Challenge Coin to Chris' twin sister. "Hound" presented a PGR Challenge Coin to Chris' mother, and "Koolstick" presented two PGR Challenge Coins to Chris' two younger brothers.

One final prayer, and it's over. The Flag Line fades away, flags are rolled up and stored, rebar pulled and returned, knowing that it will be used again, on another day, at another Church or Funeral Home somewhere in Georgia, because this is what we do. We are the Patriot Guard Riders.

As always, no mission comes together by itself, and a tip of the Ride Captains hat to each of these individuals for the assistance in pulling this together.

Dolores Berry Thrash made the phone call that got this whole thing rolling and stood the Flag Line at visitation for her friend Chris.

Lee (Vulcangunner) Love stood the Flag Line at visitation and provided the "Mission Complete" pin for Landon's bear.

Bill (Water Boy) Dowden, Mr. Flag Wagon, on top of his game as always.

Bob (Onionhead) Olander, who dug three Challenge Coins and a Marine pin out of his saddlebags.

David (Hound) Blanton, our State Captain, handled the escort, and presented a Challenge Coin.

Steve (Bendusty) Wortham, who presented a Challenge Coin.

Carrie (Hollywood) Poole, stood the Flag Line at visitation and presented the Teddy Bear to Landon.

Robert (Koolstick) Hammock, who rode escort with Hound, and presented two Challenge Coins.

Chris Pittman rode in the escort from the Funeral Home.

Kory (Kwizzle) Wilson found the best wings place in Rutledge, Ga for us to eat lunch.

It truly is a team effort, and we are blessed to have a dedicated team, but without those whose names don't make the ride report, none of this happens. They ride in, they stand the Flag line in silent respect for the fallen hero, they help you get the flags up and put away, and they ride off, with just a pat on the back and a sincere "Thank You" before they go. They are what makes this all possible, and I salute each and every one of them.

This was another mission that was 'close to home', McDonough, Griffin, Hampton, are all pretty close to my 2nd home in Jackson, and we're thankful to be able to handle these missions.

Ride Report – Atlas Jesse King, USA 08/31/2018

The text message flashed up on the phone, "Mr. King passed away. Can we get the Patriot Guard Riders for August 31?" The message was from the Commander of American Legion Post 516, Alton Head, and I knew immediately what he was talking about, and the instant response was, "We'll be there".

Atlas Jesse King would fit any one's definition of a 'living legend". When you walked into his trophy room, you couldn't help but be impressed. Trophies that were almost as tall as you were, pictures, newspaper clippings, filled every available wall space. At the height of his career, he had been a champion martial arts competitor, had fought for the world Martial Arts Championship, then became a bodybuilder, and again became a world class competitor.

Now, however, the ravages of age and some medical problems had taken their toll, and at the age of 81, the legend passed on into history. Atlas had served three years in the United States Army, before getting into martial arts, so when that text message came across the screen, the Patriot Guard Riders were honored to be able to stand for him.

As a bit of background, the men and women of American Legion Post 516 are some of the most dedicated patriots I have ever met in my life. Back in January, they had gone to Mr. King's home in Hampton, and ascertained that it was badly in need of repair, and they went to work. They raised money, they called in favors, they worked tirelessly, and had almost completed all the work, when Mr. King passed away. Undaunted, they committed themselves to finishing the job, and as of this writing, they have virtually completed the renovations and repairs, and Mrs. King will have a beautiful home to enjoy, although without her companion of many years.

Friday, August 31, dawned gray and cloudy. You cross your fingers and pray that the weatherman is correct with his "30%" chance of rain. But things are looking up when you pull into Food Depot's parking lot, and there are a half dozen bikes already there, and more on the way. Also, glad to see no less than five of Henry County PD's finest, and they've been joined by Newton County Sheriff's Deputy, JD Redlinger, who is something of a living legend himself among the motorcycle and motor officer community.

Our own "Hi-Tech Redneck", aka David Andrews, has already arrived with his specially outfitted Suburban with the slide out passenger seat, and he is carrying Mrs. King in his vehicle, so as to make it easy for her to get in an out. After greeting her, and expressing our deepest condolences, we have a short mission briefing, we say the Pledge of Allegiance, have a short prayer, and then it's helmets on, gloves up, the blue lights erupt with the accompanying sirens, and the procession is rolling.

Getting a front row seat to watch Henry County's motorcycle officers, assisted by Deputy Redlinger, handle Friday morning traffic was worth getting up for. These guys are smooth, professional, and watching them at work is similar to watch a well-choreographed ballet. They move in and out, never seem to miss a thing, cover every intersection, and roll us safely into the funeral home in Griffin, where Mr. Kings remains have already been placed in the hearse, awaiting our arrival.

We have some time to spend before heading north to Hampton, where Mr. King will be laid to rest, so it's time to swap some stories, take advantage of the facilities, and get the lineup for the procession worked out with the LEO's and the funeral director. But even with the most explicit directions and instructions, people sometimes pull out before they were supposed to, and you just shrug your shoulders and roll with it. "Semper Gumby". It's our unofficial motto. Always flexible.

Henry County's finest are working their magic again, clearing a path for us up one of the busiest highways around, and even though it's a divided highway, traffic on the opposite side almost universally comes to a halt, as good Southerners know to respect a passing funeral procession. It was truly gratifying to see this level of respect, and it made a lasting impression on the family as well.

A right turn onto Hwy 20, and we roll on. Left turn, past the Hampton City Limit sign, then another left right left jog takes us past the Senior Center where Mr. King used to go, as some of the staff and residents, including "Hi-Tech's" dad, who was a bomber pilot in WW II, greet us waving small flags.

Another left, pass in front of the now almost completely renovated home that Mr. King will never see, around the curve, and Henry County is lined up across the road, we have arrived. Right turn into the cemetery, down the hill, past the waiting tent, and then turn back up hill. Park the bike, kickstands down, peel off all the safety gear, head downhill where Jimmy White is waiting with flags, and take our positions surrounding the tent on two sides. About this time, you realize that the sun has decided to make its presence felt, and the slight breeze is extremely welcome.

The Post 516 Honor Guard calls everyone to attention as the Army Honors Team solemnly carries the urn and a folded flag to the small table in front of the tent. The minister says a few words, then one soldier holds the folded flag in front of her, all rise, and the warm Ga air rings again with those haunting, and sorrowful notes that we have heard so many times. The last note seems to hang in the air for an inexplicably long time, and then silence. The second soldier joins the first, they slowly unfold the flag, snap it flat, and slowly, patiently, refold it with honor and dignity. The flag is presented to his widow, she is weeping as the Sargent steps back, raises a perfect salute, pivots and marches off. A Patriot Guard challenge coin is presented, courtesy of one of our Mentors, Bob Olander, aka "Onionhead".

The minister says a few words, "ashes to ashes, dust to dust," then several of Atlas's colleagues got up to speak. A former sparring partner talked about how they used to train, said Atlas had the hardest punch of anyone he'd ever sparred with. I couldn't help but think about how fleeting fame was for this man, at his height, he had performed in stadiums and coliseums in front of thousands of fan, and yet, today, as he is being laid to rest, only a handful of family, and a few friends are here to cheer him on. Really was a sad day, in many respects.

The service is over, the Flag line quietly fades away. Handshakes and "thank you's" from many of the Post 516 guys. They've got dinner ready over at the King house, but most of us have other commitments and have to decline their generous offer. Flags get rolled up, static flags and rebar are pulled, put away. Handshakes, hugs, pat on the back, "see you next time", because this is what we do, and occasionally, we get to say "good-bye" to a man who truly was 'larger than life".

Rest in Peace, Atlas Jesse King, your mission here is complete.

Respectfully submitted,

David (Wild1) Shreckengost

Ride Captain

Patriot Guard Riders.

A few weeks later, the Patriot Guard Riders were asked to honor another "larger than life" American Hero. He may have served closer to home, but to me, he is still a Hero.

Ride Report – Sheriff David "Bill" Lemacks, Aug. 10/11, 2018

When you wake up in the morning, and there is a text message on your phone that says " Call me as soon as you get this" you know it's not good, because the message is from Officer Jackson, who works at the Clayton County Sheriffs Dept, and is also a Patriot Guard Rider. Your first thought is that a law enforcement officer has been killed or injured, but fortunately, a quick scan of the morning news sites did not indicate any such event had taken place, so there's nothing left to do but hit the button, and find out what's going on

A law enforcement officer had passed away, and it was the retired Sheriff of Clayton County, a man known to all as "Bill". A big man, with a big legacy, he had made a career out of law enforcement, He was one of the first members of the Clayton County Fugitive Task Force, which is not an easy job. He took over as Sheriff in 1983 and held that position until 1996, when he retired from the Sheriff's Dept, and went to work for the Georgia's Sheriff's Association, aiding law enforcement officers across Georgia. That's just the type of man he was.

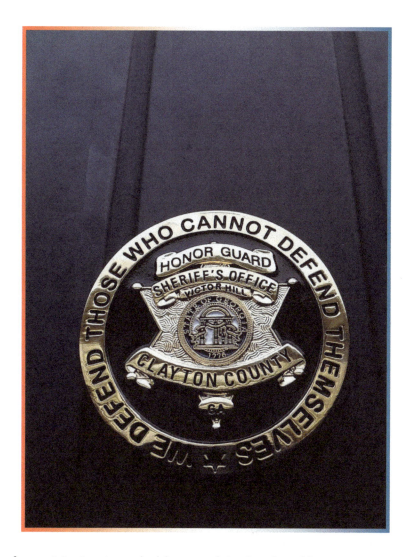

Standing a flag line for a visitation is probably one of the hardest things to get people to do, especially on a Friday night, but there were already enough folks standing in the parking lot, and more arriving, that I sent Hollywood aka Ride Captain Carrie Brand Poole, to her house nearby to get more flags, a nice problem to have. Thirteen patriots laid aside their other plans, and came and stood under the massive awning of this red brick funeral home, so that no one was in the sun, and a slight breeze made the two hours pass rather pleasantly. Many of the visitors took time to say "thank you", and even the Sheriff's son came out to the portico to express his thanks for our being there for his dad.

Two hours pass slowly, the sun sinks lower, and finally is swallowed up by cloud cover, but no one is complaining. The current Sheriff arrives, and thanks everyone present as he makes his way inside to comfort the family. Sheriff Lemacks had been a mentor to current Sheriff Victor Hill, and Sheriff Hill wanted to make sure that his friend received all the honor that he was due.

Finally, the hours have passed, and the flag line quietly makes it way to the back-parking area, where bikes and trucks and cars await. Flags are rolled, handshakes, hugs, slap on the back, "let's go eat", "see you tomorrow" is the next question, and most but not all answer in the affirmative.

Saturday morning dawned bright and clear, and the promise of a hot day could already be felt in the air. Arrived at First Baptist Church, Jonesboro, shortly after noon, to find Jimmy White and Bill Dowden were already hard at work, putting out static flags in front of the church. We didn't count them, but First Baptist Jonesboro is not a small church, and they had the front entrance well covered, which took more than a few flags. Even as the last flags are going up, Hollywood rides up, posse in tow. Seems that she had been standing in for another ride captain, Allen (Rocky) Watson, who had made the mistake of answering his phone at 2:30 in the morning, and was flying a big jet plane to NY for Delta.

But, Patriot Guard Riders, we're good like that, Semper gumby, and roll with it. So, she covered the departure from the funeral home, then followed the SWAT team to the church Knowing the arrival of the hearse was imminent, we grabbed flags and took up positions on either side of the drive, and rendered honors as the hearse passed by. The SWAT team moved with practiced precision, and lead by a bagpiper, carried the body of the Sheriff into the cavernous auditorium of First Baptist Jonesboro.

There was still plenty of time before we needed to set up a flag line, so a retreat to the shade was in order. Waiting is probably one of the hardest things we do. Your mind is going in all different directions, all the other places you could have been, things that you need to be doing, are all running at ninety miles an hour. But, despite all that, in your heart, you know, this is where you are supposed to be.

Time to set up the flag line. Hollywood and Joe man the two center doors to the church, Kevin and Bob are on opposite sides of the entryway, Jimmy, Bill, Raul, and yours truly stand in front of the massive white columns, facing the now very warm sun, and it didn't take long to decide that the shade under the entryway was a much more inviting place to stand. And stand they did, as a steady stream of visitors and law enforcement personnel made their way inside. Wasn't close enough to read all the patches and badges, but needless to say, law enforcement officers from across Georgia were there to pay final respects to a man they knew and admired.

The Masons have assembled in the church lobby, and when we see them file into the sanctuary, we know the service is about to start, and the flag line quietly disappears. The flags are quickly rolled and stashed away, then comes the task of removing all those beautiful static flags, that made such a glorious impression. Flags come up easy, rebar, not so much, but with many hands at work, it gets done quickly. Then it's on to the cemetery, but a stop at the nearby Quik-Trip is in order, as the crew is hungry.

A couple hotdogs, a cold Coca-Cola, and all is right with the world. We roll on down to the family cemetery, which is located smack in the middle of a residential sub-division. What type of sub-division you ask? The type that when the Sheriff's Dept went door to door to tell people about the big funeral that was going to take place, they said there were as many people running out the back door, as came to the front door. That kind of neighborhood.

All hands pitch in, and the flags are once again shining bright on this hot Georgia afternoon. In doing some recon earlier in the week with the Sgt in charge of the Sheriffs Dept Honor Guard, he had one request for the Patriot Guard when we got to the cemetery. "Make that fence disappear" The property directly adjacent the cemetery had a wooden fence that had definitely seen better days, but a line of American flags, each less than 3 ft from its neighbor, made a dilapidated fence disappear from view.

And again, we wait. Find some shade, grab a bottle of water, tell some stories, "you remember that mission we did over in" and so it goes. The memories, the respect, it's all part of the makeup of a Patriot Guard Rider. It's almost like it's in our DNA. We remember those who stood for us, some on foreign soil, some closer to home, but we remember.

The arrival of the Funeral Home flower van, and a Sheriff's Dept bus carrying the Honor Guard is our cue that the service is over, and we quickly line up at the cemetery gate. The wail of sirens and the roar of motorcycle engines signals the arrival of the procession, as twenty-three law enforcement motor units lead the procession to the cemetery. The motor units halt on both sides of the road, the officer's dismount and salute the hearse as it passes them, makes the right turn into the small cemetery, thru the flag line, as honors are rendered, and stops beside the open grave at the back corner.

Family cars are allowed thru the gate, also, and they park along the fence at the front of the cemetery, not the one that we had covered with flags. It takes a few minutes to get the family members back to the funeral tents, Sheriff Hill and his Senior staff stand just to one side, other law enforcement personnel fill in around the tent, and occupy most of the shaded area, leaving the Patriot Guard Riders standing in the sun, but it's what we do, and we could all stand to sweat off a few pounds.

Finally, everyone is in place, the back door of the hearse opens, the Honor Guard steps forward, and the flag-draped coffin is carried to the graveside. It's a difficult position to maneuver a casket into, with the gravesite being raised up, but with the help of three additional workers, they handled it well. The minister has a few words of comfort for the family, another minister leads in prayer, then two female deputies step forward, raise the flag, step to the side and hold it aloft.

Commands ring out from the other side of the cemetery, and the quiet afternoon air is shattered by rifle fire. Again, "Fire", and then a third volley. Silence. Then, those notes, the ones that we've heard many times, those notes that never fail to bring tears to the eyes, they seem to almost float across the many tombstones and gravesites, falling slowly on our ears, and reminding us that another hero has gone to his eternal home. As the last note fades away, the two deputies snap the corners of the flag, bring the corners together, another fold, and then the slow precise folds, that result in a three-corner symbol that dates back to the American Revolution. The last fold is made, one deputy salutes, and marches away, the other turns and hands the flag to Sheriff Hill, who kneels in front of a crying widow, says a few words of condolence, and marches away.

At the edge of the street, a radio tone sounds, and we hear the dispatcher, "Radio to 701", the call is repeated, and there is no response. The dispatcher then goes on to say that "701 has answered his last call" and gives a brief rundown of Sheriff Lemacks' career. Last call is always a difficult moment and it seemed to have powerful impact on the assembled family.

The Masons have the last word, and the Masonic ceremony is simple, but brimming with meaning and symbolism. A glove was laid on the casket, and I believe a rose as well. It was difficult to hear from our position, but the depth of the Masonic brotherhood was very obvious in the manner and bearing of the Masons that were present. A final prayer, and the Masons are done, the Sgt in charge steps forward,

"All uniformed personnel, DISMISSED".

The flag line files back to the flag wagons, roll up your flag, grab a bottle of water, "man its hot", we leave the static flags for a few minutes, until the family starts to drift away, then the process of getting up flags and pulling up rebar happens all over again. Get the flags rolled, rebar goes on the right side, close the door, handshakes, hugs, "thank you for coming" "see you next time", "careful going home". And the mission is complete.

Thank you's to Bill Dowden and Jimmy White for bringing enough flags to make a fence disappear. Carrie (Hollywood) Poole, for pinch hitting for Rocky, Bob, Joe, Kevin, Raul, ya'll did a great job, made it look good. Proud of each of you, proud to stand beside you, proud to call you friends. You are the Patriot Guard Riders, and you make this all happen.

Respectfully submitted,
David (Wild1) Shreckengost
Ride Captain, Patriot Guard Riders

The next mission was a lot closer to home than I would like, even though Athens, Ga. Is a pretty good ways from Jackson, it was still too 'close to home'.

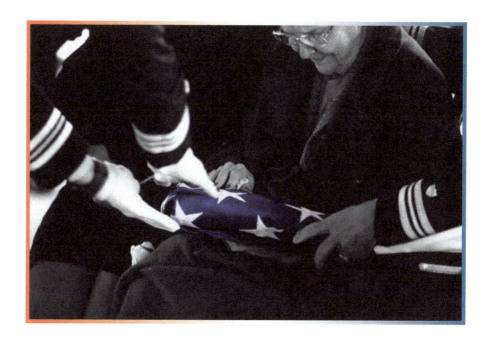

Ride Report – Charles J. Madurski Oct. 28, 2018

It was the mission, that wasn't a mission, but it was a mission nonetheless. It all began on a Thursday in August of 2018, with a text from my sister, Sarah. Her husband, CJ, as we all called him, had gotten "the long face" from the Dr, and she said they would find out on Monday what his approximate "check out" date would be. I was busy, as I almost always am, as most of us are.

Thursday night was Biker Church, Friday night we had visitation for former Clayton County Sheriff "Bill" Lemack, Saturday was the funeral service for the Sheriff. Sunday, Kay and I were at our church in Albany, then Monday it was back to work at the hospital, and I usually work late on Monday, since I get a late start. Tuesday night we have practice with the praise band at Redeemed Biker Church, so I thought, Wednesday, I will go see CJ on Wednesday after work. We'll sit down, talk, reminisce, remember the "good old days". Yup, Wednesday it is. We're gonna have a good time then.

Wednesday never came. About 7:30 pm on that Monday night, my niece Janelle, CJ's daughter called, and told me that her dad had taken his last breath as they were loading him in the ambulance to take him home. While I regret that Wednesday never came, I am at the same time glad to know that CJ is in a much better place, his body is no long eaten up with disease, and one day, I shall see him again.

Arrangements for what my sister called, "CJ's Thanksgiving Service" called for a service at St. James UMC in Athens on Sunday, Oct. 28, at 3 pm. On Saturday, Oct. 27, there was a family reunion with some cousins flying in from the left coast at my sister's house in Western New York. A quick check with Delta, yes, there is a flight from Buffalo to Atlanta at 6 am on Sunday, Oct. 28. Okay, book it.

When I had first talked to my sister about having the Patriot Guard Riders there, she thought that would be a good idea, but didn't really understand that for most missions, we don't participate in the actual service itself. We escort the hero, we escort families, we do flag lines, we do graveside flag lines, but we don't stick around for the service. I say "we", referring to the Patriot Guard as a whole, because I knew that I was definitely going to be involved in this service.

After several discussions, she decided that an escort to the church would be nice. She had CJ's ashes, and would be carrying them with her, and I assured her that it would be no problem getting bikes to come ride an escort. Having said that, and knowing I was going to be in NY for the four days proceeding, it was time to enlist some help.

On Oct. 5, the Patriot Guard assembled in Canton Ga, to pay final respects to one of our own, Dan "Irish" O'Keefe, and while at the mission, I pitched the escort to NW Ga Asst State Captain, Doug Smith, who promptly introduced me to Nathan Lippert, who is one of our mentors, and put Nathan in the driver's seat. A couple of weeks flew by without me giving it much thought, I was busy, as I usually am, then come the text from Nathan, "Like, what are we doing?" Let me check with my sister, I'll get back to you. Okay, I need six bikes to be at my sister's house no later than 2 pm on Sunday. Nathan's response, "You got it".

The man was true to his word. I had deliberately left early to get to my sister's, I was not about to be late. Passed Steve Wortham as I came into Watkinsville, going the other direction. Hadn't been at my sisters for 10 minutes when Steve rolled in from the opposite direction. Seems he was taking the scenic route. Nathan and his better half rolled up shortly thereafter, with another in tow, two more bikes rolled in to fill out the quota, and the mission was on.

Had a short briefing, and told these riders my story about Wednesday, and not getting to see CJ, and almost made it thru without choking up. Almost. I've done about 500 missions with the Patriot Guard, but this was the first one that was part of my family, and it wasn't going to be easy. But getting a bear hug from a guy whose ride name is "Standing Bear" helps a lot in situations like that. Thanks, Nathan.

Car doors slam, I get the high sign from Sis, V-twin motors roar to life, and we're off. Steve takes the lead, as he's most familiar with the area, and it's down the hill, over too many speed bumps, then left turn onto the highway. Another turn, left at the light, down the hill, then back up, over the rail road tracks, right turn, under the expressway, left turn, one more right, and we're working our way up the hill to the church, where that Flag Wagon man extraordinaire, Mr. Bill Dowden, has outdone himself.

Beautiful red white and blue flags seem to be everywhere, along the street, lining both sides of the entrance to the church, all the way to the steps, the afternoon sun and a little breeze, and your heart swelled with pride. It was beautiful.

Get the bikes parked, cars parked. Hand CJ's cremains to the Air Force Honor Guard, and they carry him inside as we render honors. The rest of the family files in, with Patriot Guard Riders lining both sides of the entrance. The family gathers in the vestibule, the minister has prayer, the doors close as the music begins, and this is where most of my Ride Reports end. The Patriot Guard Riders gather up the flags, they pull the rebar, they shake hands and hug, "careful going home", "see ya next time", and they ride off into the sunset. Not today, Kemosabe, this Ride Captain still has work to do.

My sister had billed this as a "Thanksgiving Service" and that's exactly what it was. Thankful for CJ, for his service to our country in the United States Air Force, thankful for his service to sick patients in a number of hospitals where he had worked as a nurse. Thankful for his church service as well, and for the testimony that he left behind. My sister had asked me to read Psalms 46, which was CJ's favorite scripture passage, but before I did, I had to tell a packed church about not getting to see CJ on Wednesday, and remind them the when the Bible says that "tomorrow is promised to no man". That is exactly what it means.

Got in my scripture reading and returned to my seat. The remainder of the service seemed to pass rather quickly, and then it was time. A hush descended over the church as two very sharply dressed Air Force Sergeants walked down the center aisle. They picked up the flag that was resting against the urn, slowly and carefully unfolded it, then with a snap that was quite audible, spread it wide. They held it aloft for a few seconds, then slowly, deliberately, precisely, refolded it into the familiar triangle. It is held aloft again, passed from one Sergeant to the other. The first salutes, pivots, and marches back up the aisle. The second faces the congregation and ask everyone to rise for "military honors".

From the back of the church come those familiar notes, seeming to float over the assembly like a faint autumn breeze. Twenty-four notes, we've heard them many times before, but this, this is for CJ, and the notes seem to go straight thru your heart. The last note fades, the Sergeant turns, kneels before Sarah and places the flag in her lap. "On behalf of the President of the United States, etc., etc., token of our appreciation for your loved one's faithful service". It was the first time I had seen my sister cry since CJ had passed. A final prayer, and the congregation sings one final song as the family departs.

Charles J. Madurski, United States Air Force Veteran, it was my pleasure to know you, it was my honor to escort your remains to the church for your final service, I look forward to the day when we shall once again meet face to face in the Fathers House. Until then, Godspeed.

A tip of the Ride Captains hat to Nathan "Standing Bear" Lippert, he did all the heavy lifting on this one, Thank you, my friend. Steve Wortham, Robert Drumm, R.D. Walker, thank you for taking time on a Sunday afternoon to escort CJ, he would have loved it. Bill Dowden, all I can say is, "You da Man". Bill is always there when I need him, and on this autumn Sunday, he had placed an awful lot of flags around that church, and it looked awesome. My sister is still talking about it. Gentlemen, thank you all from the bottom of my heart, you are the Patriot Guard Riders, and I am honored to stand beside you.

Respectfully submitted,

David (Wild1) Shreckengost,

Ride Captain

Patriot Guard Riders.

My last mission for the year was also 'close to home ', except this one was close to the SW Ga hideout, and was a very short notice, but a very gratifying one, nonetheless.

Ride Report – Howard Summerell, USAF, Albany Ga. 19 Nov, 2016

Patriot Guard mission request come at all hours of the day and night, but this is the first time I was elbows deep in applying some deck coating to two portable stages I had built for the hospital. Try to wipe all that stuff off your hands and answer the phone before it stops ringing. Didn't make it, had to call her back. "Hill, at Mathews, wants to talk to you". I knew what was coming.

Howard Summerell, United States Air Force Veteran, Vietnam Service Ribbon, had passed away, and the family would like the Patriot Guard to stand for him. Okay, no problem, when is the service? Tomorrow, 11 am. It's 9:30 am. Okay, let me see what I can do.

If you need something in Albany, Ga. that's related to veterans and motorcycles, and you need it fast, the first person you call is Ray Humphrey. If Ray can't help you, you are beyond help, and when Ray told me he'd be there, and round up some of his guys, (American Legion Riders Post 335, Sylvester, Ga) I knew things were looking up.

Had to locate a computer that wasn't on the hospital network (which blocks me from yahoo) but thanks to a friend in IT, got the mission up to national for posting on the PGR website. Then it's change all your plans for Saturday, but that's just how we roll.

Saturday morning dawned foggy and overcast at the SW Ga hideout, and your first thought is, great, nobody is coming out in this weather, but by 9am, when MysticK and I rolled out the driveway, a beautiful autumn day was upon us. Two doors down, we pulled into her mothers' drive, and 87 yr old Bernice Lee was headed to her first PGR mission.

Arrived at the cemetery an hour early, the hearse and casket were already present. Kay helped me put out static flags, and then you wait. One by one, motorcycles and cages pulled in, until we had 11 Patriots standing for a man they had never met, on very short notice.

A late request from the funeral director regarding folding the flag, and Ray Humphrey and the American Legion Riders again stepped to the rescue. A stiff wind had begun to blow across the dusty cemetery, and flags were standing straight out. A rather talkative minister finally stepped aside, and the Legion Riders stepped forward to flank the casket. Salutes are rendered, the flag is lifted, and slowly, precisely folded. Ray, as Commander of the Sylvester post, presented the flag to Howards son, crisply saluted, and marched back to the flag line.

A Masonic ceremony followed, and then, it's over. Another veteran has taken his place in the ranks of those who have gone before, and the flag line quietly fades away. Flags are rolled up, packed away, handshakes, hugs, "see you next time". Because as long as men like Howard Summerell continue to serve their country, the Patriot Guard, and the Legion Riders will be there to honor their service.

Respectfully submitted,
David (Wild1) Shreckengost
Ride Captain, Patriot Guard Riders

It was a year of missions that were 'close to home', at least one of them was too close. But being on the other side of the flag line helps you to see things from the point of view of the families that we serve, and helps to underscore the importance of what we do, and trying to make sure, because, as we often say in the Patriot Guard, "we only get one chance to do it right".

CHAPTER 12 – 2019

THE MISSION CONTINUES –

The year 2019 began as most do, busy working a full-time job, and somehow the timing for RCing a mission just didn't seem to work out. While there were missions that we attended, we were not in charge, and sometimes, that's okay. Then an opportunity pops up, and it turns into a very memorable mission. This was one of those.

Ride Report – Thomas Earl Cummings, May 2, 2019

Wow, that was awesome! Sometimes, as a Ride Captain, you walk away after a mission, and you think to yourself, "Wow, that was awesome". This was one of those missions.

On an absolutely perfect spring day in Georgia, an estimated 250 people came to a cemetery in Griffin, and stood in silent respect as a man that the vast majority of them had never met, was laid to rest with all the honor and dignity that the Patriot Guard Riders, the Combat Vets MC, and the United States Army Honor Guard could give him.

All the information we had on Thomas Earl Cummings was that he had served his country long ago, in a faraway place called Vietnam, but apparently some of the 'demons of war' followed him home, and he fell on some hard times, and lived out his final days homeless, on the streets of Griffin, Ga, where he was hit by an automobile while crossing the street, and passed away three weeks later, with no family present, and what family he did have, wanting nothing to do with him.

Middle of the week missions are always difficult, most of us have this little thing called a J-O-B, and we like to keep a roof over our heads, and food on the table, so it isn't always easy to take on a mission mid-week, but this one just struck a chord, not only with me, but with a lot of others as well.

It began, as so many missions do, a message gets passed along, this one coming from the Marine Corp League: would the Patriot Guard Riders come and stand for this homeless veteran? And of course, the only answer is, yes, we will. The usual myriad of phone calls, the funeral director wants to know how many bikes are going to be there, who's available with flags, details get worked out quickly, the mission gets posted on our national website, and also on our Facebook page, and then you wait.

Huggy Bear, "I'll be there", Bees, "Where do you want me, and what time"? Rocky, "I was going to sleep in, but I can nap after, I'll be there". Hi-Tech wants to know if he can leave in time to get to work. One after another, they check in. Dennis Scott – "I'm in Nashville, I'm leaving tonight so I can be there tomorrow". That's just the character of these people we call the Patriot Guard Riders. Jimmy White couldn't be there, so his wife Pat brought the flags that waved so beautifully in the bright Georgia sunshine. It truly is a team effort, and we have a great team in Georgia.

It's always a good sign, when you pull up to the cemetery early, and there are already 3 bikes waiting on you. Put out two flags at each entrance, then scout out the grave site. Static flags here, set up the flag line here, then move to the right once the service starts, so that the Marine Corp League Firing Party has a clear line of sight. Little details, but ones that make the mission go smoothly.

Then we wait. We do a lot of that in the Patriot Guard. Many missions are almost a family reunion, some of these people we don't see unless we're in a cemetery somewhere. So this is our time to get 'caught up' on what's going on, who's got a new bike, or a new job, or a new whatever, and even as we enjoy our time, a steady stream of visitors is making their way to the Oak Hill Cemetery, to say a final farewell to a man we know very little about, other than he served his country to the very best of his ability, and that is all we need to know.

The time gets closer, the flag line forms up along the walkway here in the Veterans Section of Oak Hill Cemetery, and it isn't long until the familiar rumble of V-twin engines tells us that the procession from the Funeral Home is drawing near.

Over the hill they come, flag bikes in the front, and what a beautiful sight it was. The hearse pulls to a stop, bikes park front, back and sideways, and all quickly dismount and line up facing the hearse. There is a pause for several minutes as the funeral director gets everything organized, then, that back door opens, the Honor Guard steps forward, commands ring out, and the ashes are reverently carried to the podium under the green tent.

The flag line shifts, as the visitors press in closer to the tent, with the red, white and blue catching just enough breeze to almost sparkle in the ever-warming sun. The Chaplain is from the American Legion, and after opening prayer, reminds his audience of how this soldier died, and tells them that this need not happen again, that there are organizations that help veterans, and that we should all support them. I give him a hearty "Amen" on that one. No veteran should ever be homeless or uncared for.

Another prayer, a recitation of the 23rd Psalms, and the Chaplain steps aside. Two members of the Honor Guard gently unfold the flag that was placed next to the urn, step outside the tent, and hold it straight out flat. Once again commands ring out, and the first volley from the Marine Corp League has some of the visitors jumping. A second volley, then a third, followed by those haunting, familiar notes that have sounded the final call for so many brave men and women in the past.

The six-man Honor Guard marches up on either side of the outstretched flag, and a 6-man fold is perfectly executed. They pivot, march off in perfect formation, as the flag is presented to the Spalding County Coroner, who had been instrumental in getting the word out about Mr. Cummings, and was there to see it through to the end.

The service is concluded, visitors slowly disperse, the flag line files back to waiting flag wagon, and with all hands pitching in, 45 flags are rolled up and stowed away in record time. "Thanks for coming", "see you next time", "be careful going home", and they ride away.

For one day, they were the family for a man they had never meet, yet they came, some from far, some, not so far, but all with one mission, respect, for a man they never knew, but because he served, respect.

It was my honor to stand alongside them, for they are, the Patriot Guard Riders.

Respectfully submitted,
David (Wild1) Shreckengost
Ride Captain, Patriot Guard Riders

Little did I know what a big change was going to occur on my way back to my 2nd home after completing the escort portion of this next mission, Doug Smith, Asst. State Captain for NE Ga was the Ride Captain on this one.

DEWARD W. DUNCAN, KIA, USN, WW II
ATLANTA / MONROE, GA. JUNE 6, 7, 8, 2019

ABOUT THE MISSION:

It will be an honor and privilege to provide a Welcome Home, after 75 years, to a member of our Greatest Generation: Seaman 2nd Class Deward W. Duncan, who was KIA on January 12, 1944, at the age of 19. After 75 years, his remains will finally be home and laid to rest beside his parents.

Seaman 2nd Class Duncan, who entered the US Navy from Georgia, was stationed in Betio in the Gilbert Islands, following the capture of Tarawa Atoll. On January 12, 1944, S2 Duncan was mortally wounded during a Japanese air raid when a bomb was dropped over Betio near his tent. He was reportedly buried the same day in a cemetery in Betio, but his remains could not be identified from among the remains recovered after the war. In May of 2017, the independent investigative group, History Flight, in partnership with DPAA, located a grave site in Betio and recovered human remains. DPAA analysts identified S2 Duncan from among these remains.

This mission will consist of three parts: Hero Arrival, Visitation and Funeral/Escort.

PRIMARY STAGING DETAILS: 06-06-19

Staging time: 06:45 am

Delta Air Cargo

1600 M H Jackson Service Rd.

Atlanta, Ga 30354

Ride Captain:

Doug Smith

678 – XXX – XXXX

pgr.dougga@gmail.com

Flagwagon:

Bill "Waterboy" Dowden

Special Instructions:

Please arrive on time. Our Hero will be arriving from Honolulu at 06:56 am, and his remains are expected to be at Delta Air Cargo NLT 08:00 am. We will have a quick briefing, then stand a flag line for his arrival. From there we will proceed in a LEO escort to XXX XXXXX Funeral Home in Monroe, Ga. Upon arrival, we will stand and honor our Hero as he is taken into the Funeral Home.

Flags and Water:

Flags will be provided

If you have large bike flags, please bring them,

Water will be provided

Okay, seemed pretty straight forward to me. I asked the boss if I could have that Thursday off, and he was kind enough to assent. Rolled out a bed a bit earlier than usual, threw on a jacket, fired up the Big Red Machine (01 Victory V92c, with all the chrome) and pulled into Delta Cargo well in advance of the listed staging time. Don't remember a whole lot more about that morning, the transfer from the airplane to Delta Cargo did not take as long as was anticipated, and as best I can recall, we rolled out of Atlanta International around 7:45 am.

Had an uneventful ride out to Monroe, as we had ample LEO support, it was gratifying to see many folks standing along side the road as we passed thru Monroe. Rendered honors at the Funeral Home, and then it was, "Where are we going to eat"? It's a phrase we've heard often, because we are the Patriot Guard, and we do like to eat. So off to the IHOP we went, probably ten of us, which was about half of those who had made the trip. Had a very enjoyable breakfast, good time of fellowship with other riders, just a perfect morning going on.

Time to head back to Jackson, Jimmy (Bugman) White is going at least part of the way that I'm going, so we roll out of the parking lot together. Right turn onto Hwy 138, roll down to Walnut Grove. I took a left on Hwy 81, and waved at Jimmy as he went straight on Hwy 138. It was a perfect morning, not particularly hot, just a beautiful day, made for riding on two wheels.

Roll thru Oxford, keeping the speed right at the 35-mph limit, the police in Oxford like to run radar, cruising along, I've got the whole day off, going back to Jackson, cut the grass, nothing else to do. It's a perfect morning. Cross the bridge over I-20, City of Covington City limits, still cruising, 35 mph, no hurry, realized that there is a car pulling out from the side street on my right, and she never looked my way. Threw the handlebars to the right, and went full left side into her car.

I remember the impact, the next thing I knew I was laying almost face down on the pavement, and my first thought was, "this is not good". I did not know at the time how right I was. The Covington Police were on the scene very quickly, and the Fire and Ambulance were not far behind. The EMT's did their usual triage and I was fine until they had to roll me over to get on a back board so they could load me into the ambulance. I did not know it was possible to experience that much pain. I will admit openly and without shame, I screamed. They loaded me in the ambulance, and then they're discussing, "where are we going to take him"?

The EMT supervisor very quickly said, "he's going to Grady". Oh boy. My old familiar stomping grounds. I worked in the Engineering Dept at Grady Memorial Hospital for 20 plus years, have spent many hours in the Emergency room there, but never expected to be rolled in on a stretcher.

Rolled in through the very familiar entrance, the Charge Nurse says, "Trauma 3", I know exactly where that is. Two weeks in the hospital, 8 screws and a plate holding the broken pelvis back together. And the Big Red Machine, that big, pretty bike, was totaled.

Almost 7 months later, still have no motor control in the left foot, although the Dr's keep telling me that it will come back, they just can't tell you when. Went from wheelchair, to walker, to crutches, to cane. Hopefully in the not too distant future, we can ditch the cane.

Obviously, this cut me out of taking charge of any missions for a substantial portion of the remainder of 2019. I did manage to attend a few missions, even made one up in Canton, at the Georgia National Cemetery, on crutches, but even that was tough.

Then you get that phone call, and the old drive and desire kicks in, and, well, read on.

RIDE REPORT
PRESENTATION OF FRENCH LEGION OF HONOR
LT. DAVID ANDREWS, JR.
DEC. 18, 2019

It began as most missions do, with a phone call. But this mission ended differently than any other of the over 500 missions I've been to, so that's saying something. The phone call was from our own "Hi-Tech Redneck", known in the real world as Harold David Andrews, III. He was calling to tell me that his dad was going to be posthumously awarded the French Legion of Honor for his service to the Republic of France during World War II, and would it be possible for the Patriot Guard to come and stand with him as he received this honor on his dad's behalf?

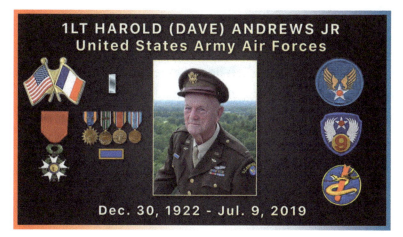

Could you possibly say no to such a request? Nope. I assured him that the Patriot Guard would be there, and they showed up in force, on a Wednesday afternoon, to stand alongside our brother, as his father received the highest honor that the French Republic can bestow. From as far south as Leary, and Warner Robbins, and as far north as Calhoun Ga, and as far East as Athens, they made their way to the Bear Creek Senior Citizens Center in Hampton Ga, not because they were going to get their picture in the paper, or their face on TV, they came to support a brother, simply because it was the right thing to do.

Hi-Tech was already there, when I rolled up, as were Bruce and Celia Tamker. This was a pretty straight forward mission, go to this room, stand with flags on both sides, and look good until the ceremony is over. No problem, we can do that. More and more Patriot Guard Riders kept showing up, and we handed out flags, and established positions on each side of the room, as visitors began to arrive for the ceremony.

It began pretty routinely, at Hi-Tech's request, the Ride Captain called everyone to their feet, and we recited the Pledge of Allegiance. Then Hi-Tech read a short description of what his dad had done in the Army Air Corps during WW II.

Then it was the French Consular's turn. He spoke about the creation of the French Medal of Honor by Napoleon in early 1800's, and how the President of the French Republic had approved the Honor for those American Servicemen who had given so much for the liberation of France between June 6, 1944, and May 8, 1945. He expressed the deep gratitude of the people of France for those who gave so much for their freedom. It was a very heartfelt speech.

Then it came time for the Consul General to pin the medal on Hi-Tech, and I don't he was quite prepared to deal with a leather vest, but, bless his heart, he stuck with it, (no pun intended) and finally got it on. Hi-Tech had a few more words to say and then the mission ended with the pop of champagne corks, as the French know how to celebrate. Everyone got a glass, and a toast was raised to Lt. Harold David Andrews, Jr. Rest in peace, Airman, and "Thank you" for your service, to the Republic of France, and the United States of America.

Thank you, Hi-Tech, for the invitation, and a tip of the Ride Captains hat to Bruce and Celia Tamker, Ruben (Tailgunner) Baumgardner, Pete (SideHack) Hefele, Nathan (Standing Bear) Lippert, Byron (Gimpy) Hall, Allen (Rocky) Watson, and his four year old Grandson, Lucas, who received his first mission pin, and a host of others, including many Legion Riders, who came with honor and respect. Thank you all, you are what makes all this possible.

Respectfully submitted,
David (Wild1) Shreckengost
Ride Captain, Patriot Guard Riders

It was truly a mission "you couldn't pass up", and although it was relatively brief, it was very meaningful, and I wouldn't have missed it for the world, even if I did have to drive a truck to get there.

And so, the mission goes on, as long as there are those who will, as RT stated so eloquently many years ago, "stand in the gap for us", the Patriot Guard Riders will, if asked, come and stand for them. Be they Active Duty Military, Veterans, First Responders, Law Enforcement, Corrections Officers, all those who serve, we will stand in honor of their service.

There is never any charge for this service, we're all volunteers, many of us are veterans, although I am not. I tell people, "Uncle Sam did not want me", and that's another long story. But by being in the Patriot Guard Riders, and honoring those who have served, this is my way of paying back just a little bit of the debt that I owe them for the freedom that we enjoy.

Lightning Source UK Ltd.
Milton Keynes UK
UKHW051911230320
360770UK00006B/182

9 781728 348162